A
CLOUD OF
WOMEN

A CLOUD OF WOMEN

THE POWERFUL CONNECTION BETWEEN BLACK WOMEN AND WOMEN OF THE BIBLE

GEORGIA A. HILL AND DIANE PROCTOR REEDER

VOICES
from Our Daily Bread Publishing

Requests for permission to quote from this book should be directed to: Permissions Department, Our Daily Bread Publishing, PO Box 3566, Grand Rapids, MI 49501, or contact us by email at permissionsdept@odb.org.

Scripture quotations, unless otherwise indicated, are taken from the Holy Bible, New International Version®, NIV®. Copyright © 1973, 1978, 1984, 2011 by Biblica, Inc.™ Used by permission of Zondervan. All rights reserved worldwide. www.zondervan.com.

Scripture quotations marked KJV are taken from the Authorized Version, or King James Version, of the Bible.

Scripture quotations marked NASB are taken from the New American Standard Bible®, copyright © 1960, 1971, 1977, 1995, 2020 by The Lockman Foundation. Used by permission. All rights reserved. www.Lockman.org.

Scripture quotations marked NKJV are taken from the New King James Version®. Copyright © 1982 by Thomas Nelson. Used by permission. All rights reserved.

Scripture quotations marked NLT are taken from the Holy Bible, New Living Translation, copyright © 1996, 2004, 2015 by Tyndale House Foundation. Used by permission of Tyndale House Publishers, Inc., Carol Stream, Illinois 60188. All rights reserved.

Interior design by Michael J. Williams

ISBN: 978-1-64070-257-8

Library of Congress Cataloging-in-Publication Data Available

Printed in the United States of America
24 25 26 27 28 29 30 31 / 8 7 6 5 4 3 2 1

I dedicate this book to my mother, Valerie Frances Proctor, extraordinary educator, counselor, mother, and human being, who taught me that "without the love of books, the richest man is poor." She is, thankfully, in this present cloud of women and still urges me on.

Diane Proctor Reeder

To my mother, Valentine Hill, and my grandmother Mary Johnson, who taught me to believe that God moves through the lives of women who trust Him. And to the mothers who prayed for me before I was born because God moved through them too.

Rev. Dr. Georgia A. Hill

CONTENTS

PREFACE

I still remember the feeling when my friend Diane read her book *A Diary of Joseph* to a room full of widows. Love and tears and pain and triumph—all of those emotions filled the atmosphere that day. I did not know her late husband, Terry, but I met him through the pages of her book—a sharing, in the best possible way, of their lives together as parents and best friends, faithful Christians, and loving spouses facing his dire diagnosis.

The book discussion took place at the church that both of our families eventually joined. Diane and I were not very close then, but our sisters were. They participated in the same confirmation class at Plymouth United Church of Christ in Detroit, interacted in the same social groups, and have remained close friends through college and marriage, work life, and social life.

Our parents were friends too. The four of them served together in an outreach ministry at a local nursing home providing a brief worship service on Sunday mornings. They were the preacher, the choir, the ushers, and the pianist for people who could no longer leave the building to attend church. They would tell stories of speechless people who still sang hymns and memories raised to life in Scripture recitation and prayer.

As big sisters, Diane and I were frequently called "fashion outlaws" by our younger sisters. We were joined in kinship by ugly long coats and strange shades of lipstick. They loved us, though, through teary-eyed laughter and their need for big-sister faith seasoned by trouble and time.

I really got to know Diane when she became the accompanist

for the praise team that sang during Friday Night Praise and Worship, an informal worship service that was organized shortly after I became ordained at Plymouth as associate pastor. After the service folks gathered to eat chicken wings, salad, and cookies. I discovered that Diane was a woman of great faith who'd written a book at the bedside of her gravely ill husband, reenvisioning his life as promise and fulfillment. Inspired by the maturity of her faith and the skill of her writing, I was happy to make the arrangements for that book discussion that comforted and motivated a roomful of widows.

Since that time Diane has spoken at African American history classes I've taught at Wayne State University. She has shared her writings on Black women playwrights at the book club I attend, and I have had the joy of participating in two of her plays, once as a dancer and once as an actress. I took great joy in playing a contemporary version of Hagar, complete with thigh-high boots and big, big hoop earrings!

Over the years we have discussed the concept and the various iterations of her play *A Cloud of Women*, noting that it is not easy to find stories about Black women of faith. As members of a group of Black Christian leaders, we have witnessed the opening of doors of opportunity for Black women at the same time that we lament the dearth of published works recounting their stories. After all, Black women are everywhere: in the courtroom and the kitchen in churches, in classes teaching kids, in pulpits preaching sermons, in countries serving as missionaries, and in business as CEOs—and yet the next generations will not be able to read about them unless the books are written.

> Therefore, since we are surrounded by such a great cloud of witnesses, let us throw off everything that hinders and the sin that so easily entangles. And let us run with perseverance the race marked out for us, fixing our eyes on Jesus, the pioneer and perfecter of faith. For the joy set before him he endured the cross, scorning its

shame, and sat down at the right hand of the throne of God. Consider him who endured such opposition from sinners, so that you will not grow weary and lose heart. (Hebrews 12:1–3)

The Bible mentions two women in this "cloud of witnesses": Sarah, the grandmother of Jacob (God later named him Israel), and Rahab, the prostitute. An unlikely pair in the eyes of the world, but to God, women who were equally "commended for their faith" (11:39). This book will take you on a journey to reimagine other lives of women, past and present, who hold a present or future place in that cloud.

So here we are, an author and a preacher, family friends, and Christian women praying that these true stories of faith will inspire your own. Parallel lives of Black women, many of whom you may know about but may never have considered how their lived experiences echo historical biblical figures like Esther, Tamar, Eve, Abigail, and so many unnamed women. Lives lived in the unquenchable hope of a living God.

Rev. Dr. Georgia A. Hill
Pastor, LifeChurch Riverside, Detroit

INTRODUCTION

They are your ancestors, you know
By birth, by blood, by culture, by faith.

A Cloud of Women play

In 1996 I began a writing journey that poetically imagined a select number of biblical women. I wondered about their lives. How did they feel about the things that happened to them? What would be a quintessentially human response? I put those thoughts down to paper, and the ultimate result was a play I called *A Cloud of Women*. The biblical characters expanded from eight to fifteen and beyond.

Since the play's debut in its infant form, every single character has been portrayed by a Black woman.

For many years the movies depicting the dramatic events recounted in the Holy Bible had one historical flaw: all the African and Middle Eastern characters were played by White people. For a while that was not a problem. Black families and White families alike would sit around the black-and-white television set and watch *The Ten Commandments* and *The Greatest Story Ever Told* and not blink an eye about the historicity of the retellings.

That has changed, but slowly. Even as late as 2014, the movie *Exodus*, directed by Ridley Scott, chose White actor Christian Bale for the character Moses. Sigourney Weaver played an African queen. In 2006, the movie *Color of the Cross* depicted Jesus as a Black man. On the *Today* show website, the movie is described as "the first representation in the history of American cinema of Jesus as a black man."[1] This is not quite accurate, as there have been lesser-known films where the role of Jesus was played by an African American, but certainly this film placed the issue of race in biblical films front and center in the public square.

This is not a phenomenon unique to the United States. In Japan Jesus is depicted as Japanese, and in China as Chinese. We as humans tend to depict Jesus in our own ethnic images.

For reasons too numerous to name here, this has not been as true in the African American community. Until just a few short years ago, Black families proudly displayed their framed pictures of a White Jesus in their living rooms and kitchens, right there with Dr. Martin Luther King Jr. and President John F. Kennedy. Today when you walk into a Black church, you are much more likely to see biblical characters, including Jesus, depicted as people of African descent.

This book aims at an even greater leap. It focuses on Black women, but with a twist.

The online magazine *Bustle* features the article "How Unconscious Biases Affect Black Women Today," pointing out "societal and economic structures that have consistently and deliberately excluded the beliefs and needs of black women."[2]

The article focuses on the diminishment of Black women, citing unfavorable attitudes toward "Black hair"; the increased punishment of Black girls in school (who can forget the story about the little Black kindergartner who was handcuffed by police in Florida and taken to the station?); the pigeonholing of Black women into stereotypical roles (Jezebel, mammy, angry Black woman); the double pressure to be uber-competent in the workplace; and the tendency of Black women to remain unchosen in online dating sites. If you are a Black woman, you can probably cite more of these.

My friend and coauthor, Rev. Dr. Georgia A. Hill, and I then asked: Why don't we take a further leap and see which of these women of the Bible find their echoes in women of African descent?

We found too many similarities to fully enumerate here. The amazing women of the Bible, we find, have stories just as compelling, just as dramatic, just as difficult, and just as deeply spiritual as the men. They are just largely unsung and underexplored.

We explore several of them in the pages to follow. And just as we find amazing heroes in Deborah the warrior-judge, Puah the midwife, and Rizpah the concubine, we discover their parallels in Fannie Lou Hamer and Marian Wright Edelman and Sybrina Fulton today. We found ourselves pulling from women who made history years ago and women who are making history today and every day.

Our offering to you is to reimagine Black women with a richer, more vivid, and beautiful portrayal. And what better way to imagine us than by holding ourselves up to a biblical mirror?

Come with us on this journey. See if you can find yourself in these pages. We pray that you will. In fact, we are sure that you will. But even more, we pray that you will find something else: that you are not alone. That El-Roi—Hebrew for "the God who sees" (Genesis 16:13–15)—walks with you and is looking to bless you and make you a blessing.

We want to close this introduction with excerpts from a spectacular sermon by the late Rev. Prathia Hall (1940–2002). She talks about African American women in particular. Her words set the tone for every chapter in this book and reflect our own sentiments about what impact we pray this book has.

> The historical work of African American women has been survival of the race. Just check the record if you don't believe me—you will find throughout his story that whenever the race is in trouble, Black women spring into action and take on every demon in hell to protect our children and preserve the race.
>
> There is a marvelous page of history right from the Women's Mission Society that is a part of our heritage. In the darkest hour in the lives of African American people, those dark hours

after Reconstruction had been betrayed when the Ku Klux Klan was rising and riding, when the Night Riders were lynching and burning, that period that has been called the nadir in African American history. Baptist women, Black and White, joined together in a group called the Bible Bands. And these mission women—they were not like women in mission societies in so many of our churches—got up early every morning. The first thing they did was to take care of their own homes. They packed their bags. The first thing to go into the bag was the Bible. They intended to bring the light of the gospel to some home that day. The next thing to go into the bag was the primer, for they intended to bring the light of literacy to some home that day. And then they would put a little detergent in the bag. It was probably some of that old lye soap. But these missionaries with a mission were not so high and holy that they were no earthly good. When they got to a house and the house was not clean or healthy, or there were a lot of children and the mother was overwhelmed, they would get down on their own knees and scrub that floor and clean that house and teach that mother how to make nutritious meals out of little or nothing and take care of her family. And they put a little medicine in the bag. The kind that grandma knew about. I remember my son [had a bee sting] and, why, we went to the doctor [and it took two weeks for him to heal] and the doctor said bee sting could be fatal, and the next time we were visiting my mother's home and my boy was stung and I was out of my mind and my aunt didn't ask a question, didn't speak a word. She took a walk around the house to some bushes, and she came back with some leaves. She rubbed them on [his] eyes. That was twenty-two years ago. . . .

The Bible Bands took some healing of the mind and healing of the spirit and some healing for the body in those bags, and they went out and they beat the bushes. These women did hand-to-hand combat against sin, sickness, death, and disease. And they didn't do it with a long-handled spoon; they did it up close and personal: house to house, shack to shack, heart to heart, hand to hand, and life to life. And because of their ministry (we came out of slavery with a literacy rate of five percent because it had been illegal to teach any Black person to read or to write), thanks be to God, because of Christian women, in forty-five years, by 1910 they had turned that statistic around, and we moved from 5 percent literate to 70 percent literate. Don't tell me it can't be done! Don't tell me the shackles can't be removed! Don't tell me our children have to be functional illiterates. Don't tell me they have to be condemned to dragging irons and cuffs.

So as you view this midnight, this nightmare in broad daylight, don't despair. Just remember who you are. Just remember whose you are. Just remember the battle has already been fought; the victory has already been won. Your job is chain removal! So take on every enemy! Take on death, sickness, and disease! Do battle![3]

Diane Proctor Reeder

WHAT IS IT *REALLY* LIKE TO BE THE FIRST?

Eve / Us

Adam named his wife Eve, because she would
become the mother of all the living.

GENESIS 3:20

I am Eve . . . Mother of you all. . . . The
first to give birth. . . . It was not easy.

A Cloud of Women play

Being the first of anything cannot be easy. It can be an honor—
like the first person to win the Nobel Prize. It can catapult
someone into infamy—like Cain, the first human being to kill
another human being.

Consider God's servant Eve, a pioneer in the journey of life.
She and Adam didn't know anything. Everything she did represented the first. She was the one, really, who pointed the way for
all women, a pathfinder who experienced all the joys and all the
consequences of every aspect of life and passed that wisdom to
her unnamed daughters.

The late award-winning author Madeleine L'Engle imagines
Eve's first pregnancy. If you've had a child, I am sure you can
relate to what she wrote in *And It Was Good: Reflections on
Beginnings*:

"Adam," she said, "I'm afraid. Something strange
has happened to me. . . . What I want is some co-
conut milk."

Adam went to try and find some, and when
he got back . . . she had rolled onto her side;
with her hands she was clutching the tree roots
and she was writhing back and forth, moaning.

What was this small creature in her arms?

They had never seen a baby before. It lay there
between them in a bed shaped by the roots of the
tree, and screamed at them angrily. . . . Its open
mouth from which issued such ferocious yowls
held no teeth. The eyelids which were squeezed
close shut were sesame with a thousand wrinkles.
They knew that it looked older than anything
they had ever seen before. . . . Nevertheless . . .
she only knew that she must hold this little thing
to her and somehow keep it safe.[1]

Already, Eve had forgotten all about the pain.

The first woman, the first mother, must have been mortified
when she and Adam were banished from paradise. She must have
wondered, *What is childbirth?* when God said that she would
have pain in childbirth (Genesis 3:16). She had been tempted
by one who had been banished from heaven, and how she had
longed to have that wonderful knowledge Lucifer had promised
her. She rejoiced at this firstborn, Cain, born of love, pain, and
blood, and she must have wanted to die herself when he viciously
attacked his younger brother and caused the first death.

Adam made love to his wife Eve, and she became pregnant and gave birth to Cain. She said,
"With the help of the LORD I have brought forth
a man." Later she gave birth to his brother Abel.

Now Abel kept flocks, and Cain worked the
soil. In the course of time Cain brought some of

the fruits of the soil as an offering to the LORD.
And Abel also brought an offering—fat portions
from some of the firstborn of his flock. The LORD
looked with favor on Abel and his offering, but
on Cain and his offering he did not look with
favor. So Cain was very angry, and his face was
downcast. . . .

Now Cain said to his brother Abel, "Let's go
out to the field." While they were in the field,
Cain attacked his brother Abel and killed him.
(Genesis 4:1–5, 8)

The biblical account does not include Adam and Eve's discovery of Abel's death and Cain's brutal, violent complicity. What a
horror for them. I imagine:

Adam: "Eve, come and see. Abel is not moving,
and there is this red fluid coming out of him."
*Eve runs to the scene and drops to her knees
as she tries to lift Abel's head and it rolls back
onto her arm.*
Eve: "Abel! Abel! Can you hear me?"
*Cain looks on, sullen, eyes filled with guilt.
Adam looks at him with a flash of recognition.*
"I know that look," Adam says to Eve. "It's
the same look we gave God when He found us
clothed in fig leaves. Remember? Cain has done
this to Abel."
Eve: "So this is what God means when He
says death."

The first woman experienced everything a human being can
experience.

Eve had to have suffered some confusion on her journey. No
human mentor to guide her and warn her of the pitfalls. Only
Adam, who was as new to life as she. And God, who must have

seemed strange to her. She didn't understand His rule not to eat the fruit. She had her own ideas about things—God made her that way. He made all of us that way—all of us have the ability to think and reason.

The first woman experienced everything a human being can experience.

As we reflect on Eve, mother of all the living, we pause to consider all the others who have labored to birth children, convince husbands, fight the devil (sometimes unsuccessfully), and handle pain. But for this book, we are looking especially at Black women.

There are so many Black women "firsts" for us to think about. Bessie Smith was the first African American female pilot. Mary Jane Patterson was the first African American female to receive a bachelor of arts degree—the year was 1862, right in the midst of the Civil War. In 1968 Shirley Chisholm was the first Black US Congresswoman in history. We have seen two Black women rise to the highest levels of government: the Honorable Kamala Harris as vice president, and the Honorable Ketanji Brown Jackson as US Supreme Court justice.

Patterson, were she alive today, would be able to tell us about the outside pressures associated with being "first." She went to Oberlin College, which served as part of the Underground Railroad that ushered the enslaved to freedom in the North, and so was part of a community that was more amenable to a diverse student body. Yet even Oberlin had a separate educational track for women—a two-year degree instead of a four-year degree. Patterson defied that system and chose the more rigorous four-year track. Imagine her sitting in a class of White males and having to prove herself to her instructors and classmates that she belonged—which she did, graduating with high honors. Later, when she pursued a career as a teacher, she was promoted to principal of an African American high school but was replaced after two years once the school began to grow—with the excuse that this was a job for a man.[2]

Chisholm, too, was challenged with the sexism of the day.

Undeterred, she continued to progress politically and became the first African American woman to run for president of the United States, under her original slogan from when she ran for Congress, "Unbought and Unbossed." That slogan brimmed with personal meaning, as men in the Congress—Black and White—tried to dismiss her as a legislator and then as a presidential candidate.

Chisholm ran in the Democratic primary against infamous segregationist and Alabama Governor George Wallace, who famously encouraged Floridians to vote for Chisholm if they could not bring themselves to vote for him. Later, when Wallace was in the hospital recuperating from an assassination attempt, Chisholm decided to pay him a visit, to the consternation of some of her supporters. "The people of my district came down on me," she remembered. But she was neither deterred nor apologetic, even though she nearly lost her congressional seat. For her it was a matter of Wallace's humanity—he was a person suffering injury. "I wouldn't want this to happen to anybody," she remembered in an interview with *Smithsonian* magazine. Unbossed indeed.[3]

Being the first certainly has its ups and downs. Listen to the Honorable Lakesia Collins, Illinois state representative, talk about the ups and downs of being Ketanji Brown Jackson, the first Black woman on the Supreme Court.

"The appointment of Jackson to the Supreme Court is a blessing and a curse, as it is for every 'first Black woman,'" Collins said. "The blessing is that this feat was witnessed in our lifetime; the curse is the looming pressure of 'messing up' under this burning magnifying glass."[4]

Black women who are "the first" in the professional world are subjected to the most excruciating scrutiny. Whites and Blacks alike will often ask: "Are they qualified?" Those who are first in the sports world find even crueler responses: "Is she a man? Is she on steroids?" Or if she presents with glamour unconventional to sports figures of any color: "Why does she have to wear [long braids, long fingernails, heavy makeup]?"

Eve, too, has been subject to scrutiny over the millennia. *Why did she have to mess it up for all of us?* we think. We never stop to ask, "Just how hard was it for Adam and Eve to have the entire range of human experiences for the very first time?" or "What was it like to be responsible for the entire earth? Was it overwhelming?" Do we think, *Poor Eve. Her son killed her other son. How did she have the courage to even bring one more person into the world?*

Eve embodies the two-edged sword of being the first. I imagine her saying, "I wish you would remember me for more than just eating that fruit." I challenge us to rethink this first woman, Eve, pioneer of life. She is the template for us all.

WOMEN'S VOICES RISING

Deborah / Fannie Lou Hamer, Black Female Judges Today

> In the days of Shamgar son of Anath, in the days of Jael, the highways were abandoned; travelers took to winding paths. Villagers in Israel would not fight; they held back until I, Deborah, arose, until I arose, a mother in Israel.
>
> JUDGES 5:6–7

> My people were without vision. Sick of the Canaanite kings, who killed our children and dishonored our women. My husband and I were safe here in the hills, where the chariot wheels could not reach. But it was not enough to be safe, not for me. I called Barak, a soldier. I reminded him of how God had delivered us. I reminded him that this was our land of Promise. I compelled him to go and fight. He said he would not go without me. I surprised him: I said yes. The Canaanite king was no match for the eternal God.
>
> *A Cloud of Women* play

This Old Testament Scripture in Judges describes the one female judge mentioned in the Bible: Deborah. We'll call Deborah an unsung biblical hero because her story, as is the case of many women's stories, is not often the subject of preachers' messages.

Deborah was a judge in Israel, the highest designation of

leadership at the time. The book of Judges describes several of these persons chosen by God who were considered to be of high integrity and wisdom. Like today's judges, they provided counsel in disputes. Unlike today's judges, they were also tasked with leading the nation in war. Deborah performed both functions. She "held court under the Palm of Deborah between Ramah and Bethel in the hill country of Ephraim, and the Israelites went up to her to have their disputes decided" (Judges 4:5). In this manner her role was no different than the first leader, Moses, who ushered the Hebrews out of slavery in Egypt and into the promised land of Canaan.

But she also led Israel during a time when they were in captivity to the Canaanites, the people who lived in the land that God had promised to the Israelites. The Canaanites had a massive army that included nine hundred iron chariots, and they used those chariots to keep the nation of Israel locked away from the main roadways, making transportation for trade and communications virtually impossible. The Israelites were herded into ghettos, if you will, and the chariots made it hard for them to do anything. That oppression lasted for twenty years. Then Deborah was appointed: "Deborah first was recognized as a prophet, then as judge and leader; next in a military role [see Judges 5:15], and finally as a songstress."[1]

In other words, Deborah was a multitasker, much like women today! Imagine her leadership in a time when women were considered "less than"—less than intelligent, less than capable, only good for bearing children. Some scholars state that the Hebrew men used to thank God that they were not a Gentile, a slave, or a woman. Women were second-class citizens whose opinions were largely dismissed and disrespected.

But not Deborah. Somehow she developed the ability to pierce those misperceptions about women and lead a nation of men and women socialized to believe that women should not lead. The Scripture suggests that one way she accomplished that was by singing:

On that day Deborah and Barak son of Abinoam
sang this song:

"When the princes in Israel take the lead,
   when the people willingly offer themselves—
   praise the LORD!

"Hear this, you kings! Listen, you rulers!
   I, even I, will sing to the LORD;
   I will praise the LORD, the God of Israel, in
      song.

"When you, LORD, went out from Seir,
   when you marched from the land of Edom,
the earth shook, the heavens poured,
   the clouds poured down water.
The mountains quaked before the LORD, the One
      of Sinai,
   before the LORD, the God of Israel.

"In the days of Shamgar son of Anath,
   in the days of Jael, the highways were
      abandoned;
   travelers took to winding paths.
Villagers in Israel would not fight;
   they held back until I, Deborah, arose,
   until I arose, a mother in Israel.
God chose new leaders
   when war came to the city gates,
but not a shield or spear was seen
   among forty thousand in Israel.
My heart is with Israel's princes,
   with the willing volunteers among the people.
   Praise the LORD!

"You who ride on white donkeys,
   sitting on your saddle blankets,
   and you who walk along the road,
consider the voice of the singers at the watering
      places.
   They recite the victories of the LORD,
   the victories of his villagers in Israel.

"Then the people of the LORD
went down to the city gates." (Judges 5:1–11)

Deborah challenged her underling soldier, Barak, to partner with her to defeat the Canaanites. "Go, take with you ten thousand men . . . to Mount Tabor," she directed. "I will lead Sisera [the Canaanite king] . . . to the Kishon River and give him into your hands" (Judges 4:6–7). Barak balked at her direction. Was it because she was a woman? Perhaps not. He actually said something curious for a man, especially at that time: "If you don't go with me, I won't go" (v. 8). He had so much respect for her leadership that he felt he needed her by his side in order to win.

Deborah was a warrior. God called and equipped her that way. And so she agreed.

Women are not usually seen as warriors. But we have some African American women in our recent history who could only be described using that word.

We are indebted to *A Voice That Could Stir an Army: Fannie Lou Hamer and the Rhetoric of the Black Freedom Movement*, by Maegan Parker Brooks, for Hamer's history.

> For our struggle is not against flesh and blood,
> but against the rulers, against the authorities,
> against the powers of this dark world and against
> the spiritual forces of evil in the heavenly realms.
> (Ephesians 6:12)
>
> He trains my hands for battle; my arms can bend
> a bow of bronze. (Psalm 18:34)

Like Deborah, Fannie Lou Hamer lived under oppressive conditions. Like Deborah, Fannie's people were tired of these unfair conditions. Like Deborah, they were called to change it. When we examine the course of Deborah's and Fannie's lives, we find striking parallels.

Let's start with Fannie Lou Hamer. Born in 1917 to parents

who worked as sharecroppers and had twenty children in the deep southern state of Mississippi—a state Dr. Martin Luther King Jr. described as "sweltering with the heat of injustice and oppression" in his "I Have a Dream" speech—Hamer, like Deborah, was living under unbearably oppressive conditions.[2] Parents and small children alike were compelled by economic necessity as well as fear of physical harm or fear of death to work the cotton fields of the Mississippi Delta from sunup to sundown. The White plantation owners' "creative" accounting kept these Black families in permanent debt, even though the revenues from the sale of that cotton kept the owners well-heeled in cash and assets. The Black workers, nearly all of whose parents, if not themselves, had been enslaved, were not allowed to take part in the profits but instead were charged for all the material costs of production, including seed and fertilizer along with the cost of their meager, bare subsistence living conditions.

Hamer represented the second generation of African Americans who had not been born into slavery. As such, they were much less accepting of the conditions under which they lived.

Anthropologist Hortense Powdermaker observed in her 1930 study, *After Freedom: A Cultural Study in the Deep South,* that the children born two generations removed from slavery—the generation to which Hamer belonged—"exhibited a great deal more resentment at their station in life. They considered themselves entitled to equal treatment and were much less comfortable than their parents had been with the elaborate codes of ritual deference."[3]

Some of that discontent might well be attributed to the parents of these children. It was certainly true in the case of Fannie Lou Hamer's mother, Lou Ella Townsend, who consistently repeated to her children the empowering message that the Whites who continued to enslave them were not to be envied despite the indoctrination by the White plantation owners that Black people's condition was due to their inherent inferiority.

> Her mother's belief that black people were oppressed by no fault of their own ran directly counter to the widespread Social Darwinist

explanation of black inferiority that served to
justify the exploitative sharecropping system.
Arguing further that white oppressors deserved
no envy, Lou Ella's alternative explanation really
"sank down in" young Fannie Lou's mind.[4]

Young Fannie Lou Hamer believed her mother, not the message
of the prevailing dominant culture. No doubt Lou Ella Townsend
was repeating the message of a long line of ancestors who inculcated
in the next generation a countercultural message that strengthened
with successive generations.

In Hamer we find echoes of Deborah, who hailed, as it has
been suggested in Jewish oral history, from one of the twelve
tribes of Israel—Naphtali, to be exact. From the time that God
chose Abraham to leave his land and kinfolk and venture out to
launch a chosen people, the Hebrew community has passed down
the tantalizing, compelling, and real stories of their journey with
God across the Mideast from generation to generation. They did
it because God himself told them to:

> Listen, O Israel! The LORD is our God, the LORD
> alone. And you must love the LORD your God
> with all your heart, all your soul, and all your
> strength. And you must commit yourselves whole-
> heartedly to these commands that I am giving you
> today. Repeat them again and again to your chil-
> dren. Talk about them when you are at home and
> when you are on the road, when you are going to
> bed and when you are getting up. Tie them to your
> hands and wear them on your forehead as remind-
> ers. Write them on the doorposts of your house
> and on your gates. (Deuteronomy 6:4–9 NLT)

Like Deborah, Fannie Lou Hamer heard those commands
and stories as well. Hamer heard them from her father, preacher
James Lee Townsend. At that time the Black preacher was one

of the spiritual and cultural reference points for the community. He or she retold the ancient biblical stories that resonated with the congregation: the story of Moses telling Pharaoh to "let my people go," and the story of Jesus, who cared especially for those who were sick with disease or without hope. In the same way the Hebrew people had a shared cultural and spiritual tradition and history, African American communities had developed their own Christian tradition that affirmed their life and their worth, and that gave fire and impetus to their work on behalf of their families and their people.

Hamer was baptized in the Quiver River at twelve years old and joined a Bible study at the Stranger's Home Baptist Church. As the daughter of a Black preacher and a Sunday school–teaching mother:

> Hamer would often couple her mother's transformative lesson—that God intended for her to be black and that she should not covet the station of her white oppressor—with biblical verses such as Galatians 6:7 (NKJV), "Do not be deceived, God is not mocked; for whatever a man sows, that he will also reap." This biblical instruction, combined with her mother's wisdom, endowed Hamer with an abiding sense of divine justice, giving her the faith she needed to persevere in the face of gross inequality.[5]

But the scripture that had the greatest impact on this young girl was repeated often enough that she knew it by heart:

> The Spirit of the Lord is upon me, because he hath anointed me to preach the gospel to the poor; he hath sent me to heal the brokenhearted, to preach deliverance to the captives, and recovering of sight to the blind, to set at liberty them that are bruised, to preach the acceptable year of the Lord. (Luke 4:18–19 KJV)

That Scripture resonated with the desperately poor conditions of the Mississippi sharecroppers—conditions directly tied to an unjust and oppressive economic system that would continue for generations. Deborah, too, had believed the narrative that had been passed down through the generations since Moses led her people to the promised land. Like the Black preachers in the tradition of Fannie Lou Hamer's father, it was a message of hope and empowerment:

> When you and your children return to the LORD your God and obey him with all your heart and with all your soul according to everything I command you today, then the LORD your God will restore your fortunes and have compassion on you and gather you again from all the nations where he scattered you. Even if you have been banished to the most distant land under the heavens, from there the LORD your God will gather you and bring you back. He will bring you to the land that belonged to your ancestors, and you will take possession of it. He will make you more prosperous and numerous than your ancestors. The LORD your God will circumcise your hearts and the hearts of your descendants, so that you may love him with all your heart and with all your soul, and live. The LORD your God will put all these curses on your enemies who hate and persecute you. You will again obey the LORD and follow all his commands I am giving you today. Then the LORD your God will make you most prosperous in all the work of your hands and in the fruit of your womb, the young of your livestock and the crops of your land. The LORD will again delight in you and make you prosperous, just as he delighted in your ancestors, if you obey the LORD your God and keep his commands and decrees

that are written in this Book of the Law and turn
to the LORD your God with all your heart and
with all your soul. (Deuteronomy 30:2–10)

Deborah's song in Judges 5 reveals her deep and abiding faith, where she blesses God at every turn and speaks of her heart for the people, from the "princes, [to] the willing volunteers" (v. 9). But she did more than sing her faith: she demonstrated it. She spent the bulk of her time "in the hill country of Ephraim" (Judges 4:5), listening to interpersonal disputes and dispensing her wisdom. That in itself was an act of faith! How difficult must it have been for a woman to be in that position eleven centuries before Jesus was born.

In addition to listening to the people, she listened to God, and like the prophet she was, both relayed His messages to those meant to hear it and gave critique when there was pushback. But she went even further. She was willing to risk her life on the front lines of war in order to secure the freedom of the generation of Israelites who came after those nearly million who wandered in the wilderness for forty years.

Fannie Lou Hamer had a similar faith. Her father was a minister and she recalls hearing her mother pray over all of her children.[6] Her faith was sharpened and grew on the razor's edge of intergenerational suffering, where it cut through and elegantly simplified the demands of justice in light of the ample scriptures devoted to that topic. Her insights and ability to relate the Bible to the issues of the day made room for her as a community organizer and leader and carried her all the way to Washington, DC, and the halls of Congress by way of the civil rights movement.

> Like Deborah, Fannie Lou Hamer found herself in the midst of a man's world.

Like Deborah, Fannie Lou Hamer found herself in the midst of a man's world. It was not at all common for women to go to war as Deborah did. Likewise, it was very unusual for a woman, especially a Black woman, to assert herself and take the mantle of leadership in that movement. The speeches she made reveal a shoe-leather theology deeply rooted in the Bible she undoubtedly learned from her parents and applied in her day-to-day journey. Following is an excerpt of a speech she delivered in the fall of 1963 at a Freedom Voter ally designed by famed activists Bob Moses and Allard Lowenstein to prove the desire of Black Mississippians to participate in the electoral process:

> From the fourth chapter of St. Luke beginning at the eighteenth verse: "The Spirit of the Lord is upon me because he has anointed me to preach the gospel to the poor. He has sent me to heal the brokenhearted, to preach deliverance to the captive, and recover the sight to the blind, to set at liberty to them who are bruised, to preach the acceptable year of the Lord."
>
> Now the time have come that was Christ's purpose on earth. And we only been getting by, by paying our way to Hell. But the time is out. When Simon [of] Cyrene was helping Christ to bear his cross up the hill, he said, "Must Jesus bear this cross alone? And all the world go free?" He said, "No, there's a cross for everyone and there's a cross for me. This consecrated cross I'll bear, till death shall set me free. And then go home a crown to wear, for there's a crown for me." And it's no easy way out. We just got to wake up and face it, folks. And if I can face the issue, you can too. You see, the thing, what's so pitiful now about it, the men been wanting to be the boss all of these years, and the ones that ain't up under the house is under the bed. But you see, it's poison; it's poison for us not to speak what we know is right. As Christ said from the seventeenth chapter of Acts and the twenty sixth verse, says: "Has made of one blood all nations, for dwell on the face of the earth." Then it's no different, we

just have different colors . . . it's kind of like in the twenty-third of Psalms when he says, "Thou prepareth a table before me in the presence of my enemies. Thou anointed my head with oil and my cup runneth over." And I have walked through the shadows of death because it was on the tenth of September in '62 when they shot sixteen times in a house and it wasn't a foot over the bed where my head was. But that night I wasn't there—don't you see what God can do? Quit running around trying to dodge death because this book said, "He that seeketh to save his life, he's going to lose it anyhow!"[7]

Like Deborah, Fannie Lou knew she had a purpose that was God given. She found echoes of contemporary life in those ancient Bible stories and breathed life into them to fight for justice in the 1960s. She understood what James the disciple taught in the book named after him: Faith without works is dead (James 2:17).

Deborah was a mother in Israel and a mother of a movement. "In the days of Jael, the highways were abandoned; travelers took to winding paths. Villagers in Israel would not fight; they held back until I, Deborah, arose, . . . a mother in Israel" (Judges 5:6–7). Pastor Pam Otten writes in her *She Is Called: Women of the Bible* study, "[Deborah] saw all of Israel as her children and longed for all of her children (literal and figurative) to experience peace and security."[8]

The Bible does not say whether Deborah had children. But she calls herself a mother. She is perhaps early in a long tradition of women who, though they may not have biological children, mothered other people's children by nurturing and fiercely guarding their safety and well-being.

Fannie Lou Hamer and her husband did that too.

Hamer was childless, but not by choice. She had two stillborn children, and she was victimized by a viciously racist health-care system that sterilized her without her permission when she was forty-two. She went into the hospital for fibroid removal and came out without a uterus—as was the case with up to six out of ten Black women in the state of Mississippi at the time. The Hamers eventually adopted two children: one born of a single mother, and the other born with severe health challenges into a family of more than twenty. She speaks of her passion for her race, and especially for the children, when she says at the Freedom Vote Rally in Mississippi in 1963, "Where [can I] stand up and speak for my race and speak for these hungry children?"[9]

The struggle is real. A warrior understands that the nature of war is struggle and battle—not only with the enemy but sometimes with those who purport to be colleagues and allies. It was no different with Deborah. Yes, she had to battle the Canaanites, and they were her first priority. But she also skirmished with her soldier Barak . . . and with certain tribes of Israel who opted out of the battle even as their own lives depended on the outcomes. But she had no problem challenging both Barak and the tribes:

> In the districts of Reuben
>   there was much searching of heart.
> Why did you stay among the sheep pens
>   to hear the whistling for the flocks? . . .
> Gilead stayed beyond the Jordan.
>   And Dan, why did he linger by the ships?
> Asher remained on the coast
>   and stayed in his coves. (Judges 5:15–17)

Deborah praised the tribes that joined the battle with her and the soldier Barak and mocked those tribes and groups—Reuben, Gilead, Dan, and Asher—that exhibited reluctance and fear.

Fannie Lou would find similar challenges as she struggled to wrest justice out of the country's clenched hands. In her biography on Ella Baker and the Black Freedom Movement, Barbara Ransby says that Hamer's "way of being a black woman" forced men in the movement to reconsider their thoughts on manhood and masculinity. Her personhood also gave women a wider sense of who they were and could be as agents of change.[10]

Before these men began the rethinking process, however, they seemed to work overtime to find ways to dismiss and discredit this powerful Black woman. Her voice, with its strong southern accent and heavy use of African American Vernacular English, suggested to many of the movement workers—who had attended college and many of whom were from the North and not accustomed to the differences in pronunciation of southern speakers with their dropped *r*'s and drawn-out syllables—that she was not as intelligent as they were. Even the Student Nonviolent Coordinating Committee, considered at the time a radical civil rights organization, had college-educated members who dismissed Hamer as not relevant or not at "our level of development."[11]

The disrespect may have cut deeply into her spirit, ironically just at the time that she was fighting, alongside those who viewed her as beneath them, the oppressive regime in Mississippi. When she ventured out of the South as her fiery speeches began to garner word-of-mouth notoriety, Fannie Lou was met with arrest back in her home state of Mississippi, where she was brutally beaten and sexually assaulted by the police and her jailers, and bore the effects of the attack until her death in 1977.

Deborah's song celebrated Israel's victory over oppression. Fannie Lou Hamer, wrote one reporter, "sings as if the entire world depends on it." He noted "the power of her voice because there was a mission behind it and in it."[12] Many are no doubt familiar with the song "This Little Light of Mine." Hamer was the one who added the words "Jesus gave it to me. I *have* to let it shine." Her movement work was deeply grounded in the message of Jesus Christ passed on to her by her mother and father. In an echo of Deborah's critique of her people who would not enjoin the battle, Hamer added these words to the Negro spiritual "Go Down Moses":

Who's that yonder dressed in black? Must be the hypocrites turning back. Let my people go.

Charles Cobb, a SNCC organizer, shared,

From the back of the bus this powerful voice
broke out in song. I remember hearing "this
little light of mine" and "ain't gonna let nobody
turn me 'roun." The voice, Cobb clarifies, "was
Mrs. Hamer, until when, just one of seventeen
or eighteen people, with the power of her voice
alone, she shored up everybody on the bus."[13]

The warrior Deborah is memorialized in the book of Judges.
Hamer's legacy as a fighter is memorialized too. If you travel to
Ruleville, Mississippi, today you will find the Fannie Lou Hamer
Garden and a full-body statue in her honor. And as Parker Brooks
describes:

The memorial site where she and her husband
are buried sits on forty acres of land, adjacent
to the town's recreational center. And many of
the hundreds of houses for low-income residents
that Hamer worked tirelessly to fund still provide shelter to Ruleville residents.[14]

"Now Deborah, a prophet, the wife of Lappidoth, was leading Israel at that time. She held court under the Palm of Deborah between Ramah and Bethel in the hill country of Ephraim,
and the Israelites went up to her to have their disputes decided"
(Judges 4:4–5).

Deborah was more than a warrior. She was a judge too. And
thankfully for us, the state of Michigan, where Rev. Georgia and
I both were born, has an embarrassment of riches: strong, prin-
cipled African American female judges who bring godly wisdom
and compassion to the bench. We are going to lift up just a few
standouts because there are too many to mention.

It started with the late Geraldine Bledsoe Ford (1926–2003). She
was the first Black woman in the United States to be elected to a
judgeship. She believed that convicted offenders should receive stiff
sentences but that all defendants had a right to a full and robust

defense. She had a particular focus on making sure that Black students who were the beneficiaries of affirmative action received the support they needed to be academically successful. Her daughter, Deborah Geraldine Bledsoe Ford, now serves in the Thirty-Sixth District Court in Detroit. In 1983 mother Ford had the honor of being inducted into the Michigan Women's Hall of Fame.

The late Anna Diggs Taylor was the first Black woman to be appointed judge to the United States District Court for the Eastern District of Michigan and ultimately became the first Black woman Chief Judge as well. She made a momentous decision in 2006, holding that warrantless domestic wiretapping by the National Security Agency was unconstitutional. While her decision was overturned, it further raised the issue of whether these federal activities are legally justified.

The Honorable Denise Page Hood, former Chief Judge, US District Court for the Eastern District of Michigan (retired, now Senior Judge), followed in Judge Diggs Taylor's footsteps as African American Chief Judge for the US District Court for the Eastern District of Michigan. She adjudicated a case where she determined that egregious prosecutorial conduct mandated a reversal of a guilty verdict. "Things had happened regarding the prosecution that simply rose to a constitutional level and needed to be righted,"[15] she explained. It was a public case, and her decision was controversial. Judge Hood remained true to her conviction and made a courageous decision.

The Honorable Deborah Thomas, Judge, Third Judicial Circuit Court of Michigan, was decisive in the case of Maryanne Godboldo. Godboldo had a special-needs thirteen-year-old daughter for whom she was lovingly caring. A doctor had prescribed Risperdal as a way to control the girl's behavior, and Godboldo observed that her daughter was actually getting worse with the drug. When she expressed reservations about administering the medication, Child Protective Services intervened and threatened her with jail.

Police came to Godboldo's home, pounded on the door, and indicated that they had a warrant for her arrest. She refused to open the door, and it was suggested that she shot a gun into the ceiling of the house, though her attorney Cornelius Pitts questioned the evidentiary basis for that contention.[16]

That is where Deborah Thomas stepped in. She was called by anti–police brutality advocate Ron Scott to come and mediate the situation to avoid further escalation.

"We talked that day mother-to-mother. I asked her to come out on her porch and I promised I would come here today to walk out with her," Thomas said in an interview with the *Detroit News*.[17] By the end of the year, all child-neglect charges against Godboldo were dismissed.

Thomas may have halted a tragedy that day. She has adjudicated many cases, but on that particular day, she showed wisdom, prudence, and compassion for a mother and her child.

The Honorable Linda Parker, Judge, US District Court for the Eastern District of Michigan, addressed nine lawyers allied with former President Donald Trump facing financial penalties and other sanctions after a judge said they had abused the court system with a lawsuit that challenged Michigan's election results in favor of Joe Biden. Judge Linda Parker said the lawsuit was a sham intended to deceive the court and the public, just a few days after Mr. Biden's 154,000-vote victory in the state was certified.

Despite the haze of confusion, commotion, and chaos counsel intentionally attempted to create by filing this lawsuit, one thing is perfectly clear: "Plaintiffs' attorneys have scorned their oath, flouted the rules, and attempted to undermine the integrity of the judiciary along the way," Ms. Parker said in the opening of a scathing 110-page opinion.[18]

Parker took a strong stand during the 2020 presidential election. The decision she made took courage—there were violent forces in Michigan arrayed against the democratic process, as evidenced in the case of the Wolverine Watchmen group, who in 2020 worked on a plot to kidnap Michigan's governor, Gretchen Whitmer. Like Deborah, Judge Parker rendered wise judgment.

The Honorable Victoria Roberts in 1999 torpedoed the Michigan legislature's plan to test all welfare recipients for drugs, saying it would constitute an unreasonable search and seizure. Her decision withstood two appeals.

Roberts also initiated major projects in 2017 and 2018: the creation of a clinic, staffed by University of Detroit Mercy School of Law students, to assist low-income citizens who represent themselves in federal civil suits, and a mediation program to try to quickly resolve civil rights lawsuits filed by Michigan prisoners who represent themselves.

In 1939 a Black man by the name of Jessie Lee Bond was lynched in Arlington, Tennessee, because he had the temerity to ask a White store owner for a receipt for items he purchased. More than eighty years later, his great-granddaughter, The Honorable Kyra Bolden, made history as the first Black woman to ascend to the Michigan Supreme Court. Appointed by Governor Gretchen Whitmer, Judge Bolden said that she was compelled to "be part of the justice system" because of this act that so deeply impacted and traumatized her own family.[19]

And now, we have a shining new first: The Honorable Ketanji Brown Jackson, U.S. Supreme Court. Black women beamed with pride as she so smoothly and masterfully parried with the US Congressional representatives who tried so hard to discredit and dismiss her. She was able to ignore the media personalities, who had to strain to find a critique, even to the point of questioning her law school admission test scores despite having graduated magna cum laude from Harvard University and cum laude from Harvard Law School.

Deborah, Fannie Lou Hamer, Geraldine Bledsoe Ford, and Anna Diggs Taylor have joined the ancestors. The remaining judges mentioned are still bringing wisdom and justice as they contribute to our world. Their stories intersect through time and millennia, representing wisdom and justice that come from God.

> But the wisdom that comes from heaven is first of all pure; then peace-loving, considerate, submissive, full of mercy and good fruit, impartial and sincere. (James 3:17)

A MOTHER'S LOVE

Mary the Mother of Jesus, Her Counterparts / The Mothers of Martin, Malcolm, and James

For our "God is a consuming fire."
HEBREWS 12:29

How do you prepare for the kind of pain that gives birth? To that kind of joy? And then, to do it all over again? And to see the terror of free will. A terror nothing can prepare you for.
A Cloud of Women play

God's love is at once a wondrous and terrible thing. It winds its way inexorably through time, sometimes represented by cool running water to quench souls, sometimes as consuming fires to quench evil, sometimes as oil to anoint and spur greatness.

God's love is at once discriminating and wild. It goes where it wants to go, which is everywhere and especially to places mere humans think are inappropriate.

But nowhere does God's love show more extravagantly than in the heart of a mother. Mothers reflect God's love like a prism, every facet showing itself over time: fierce like a lion, wise like the ages, tender as a moonlit night. Like God's love, her love does not change and cannot be thwarted.

Mothers can't help but have an impact on their children, for good or evil. Society knows that. It blames the mother when the child does not succeed or thrive, much more often than it praises her when the child succeeds.

Just take another look at Eve, the first mother of the first man born to woman, Cain. She had gotten a man-child from the Lord. Before she had him, however, she was duped by the devil, who tricked her into doing exactly what God had told her and husband, Adam, not to do: eat from the tree of the knowledge of good and evil. For that one act, they brought down the whole of mankind! And then sin entered the world and Cain killed his brother and . . . see? All Eve's fault. We're all mad at Eve. "Why'd you have to go and do that?" we want to ask her.

Now contrast that with the woman Mary, mother of Jesus. She raised Jesus, the Christ! The perfect human who was both man and God in the same body. The one who spouted wisdom and knew how to take down religious hypocrites and had an answer for everyone and could see into their hearts and knew where they were. Mary raised Him!

"What child-rearing methods did she use?" said no one *ever*. We all simply assume that as the only begotten Son of God, Jesus would automatically be perfect. So why did He have a mother? What role did she play?

See? Eve gets the blame for the whole world, and Jesus's mother, Mary, gets a glance of appreciation for being so quiet and submissive. Mary was more than that.

We sanitize the Scriptures so much that we miss the context in which the stories are told. Have you ever thought about the times during which Mary was living, when Jesus was born? Let's recount.

"In the sixth month of Elizabeth's pregnancy, God sent the angel Gabriel to Nazareth, a town in Galilee, to a virgin pledged to be married to a man named Joseph, a descendant of David" (Luke 1:26–27). Mary, a Jewish young woman who would soon after this be visited by an angel, lived in the town of Galilee in northern Israel. Israel had a turbulent history—these God-chosen people who comprised a nation had decided long ago to establish a monarchy against God's own counsel, and just as God had warned, that top-down system of governing had not worked out too well. The original governing system in Israel, after they were delivered by God from their Egyptian oppressors and enslavers, was a series of judges who rose up whenever other nations were trying to invade or oppress them. Deborah was only one of those judges, as you read earlier. These judges served as warriors and were committed to keeping Israel out of other nations' control so that they could freely serve God, whom they called YHWH, pronounced *Yahweh*. In addition to not wanting to be dominated and controlled by another nation, the Israelites were committed to having no king other than God. Human domination was anathema to them. That commitment would be tested over the centuries.

Even during the period after the Israelite judges, when kings ruled instead, there were many times that would-be and sometimes successful occupiers would invade Israel and demand that they bow to their king. One of the most famous of these times was when the nation of Babylon had invaded Israel. The Babylonian king, Nebuchadnezzar, had taken Israel's best and brightest to serve his kingdom, including four young men: Shadrach, Meshach, Abednego, and Daniel. These four men bravely refused to bow to the king—they would have no king but God—and their courage was rewarded when all the king's efforts to punish them by death were thwarted with God's miraculous intervention.

Over time the invasion and conquering of Israel by other nations became almost commonplace. Sometimes they fought back valiantly, as they did around 167 BC, when the Greeks invaded.[1]

The problem was not just that Israel was being invaded—the problem was that these invading nations were imposing nothing short of cultural and religious annihilation. Not to mention that some of the Jewish leadership were collaborating, showing more loyalty and deference to their oppressors than to their own nation.

At the time Mary was engaged to Joseph, Israel was led by a king from the Hasmonean dynasty. Just a few decades before, around 63 BC, the Roman general Pompey had invaded Israel, and this dynasty "proved to be so morally corrupt and so exploitative of their own people that . . . some Jews actually welcomed him."[2]

So just before Jesus became a human being born to Mary, the Romans had taken charge brutally, sometimes slaughtering Jewish citizens and sometimes enslaving them. The kings of Hasmonean descent, who were often challenged by other family members, were equally brutal as they vied for power—the winner of what was originally intended to be a calling to spiritual leadership would often take his throne by extreme violence.

Herod the Great, who came to power in 37 BC, and was of partial Jewish descent, was one of those exceptionally brutal Jewish kings. He felt entitled, as a son born into a privileged family where his father was an appointed governor in the region, to whatever he was given—and whatever he decided to take. So heartless was he that when he thought his kingship was in jeopardy, he ordered all Jewish males under two years of age to be summarily killed—just to make doubly sure that none of them would usurp him. The Jewish historian of the period, Josephus, says that Herod's murderous grip on power included brutal enforcers—today we might call them "corrupt police"—who spied on the people, infiltrated Jewish groups dissatisfied with his leadership, tortured and made examples of those who dared to protest, and insisted on 100 percent loyalty, no excuses.

And Herod did not mind that his superiors, the Romans, were bent on obliterating Jewish culture and theology. His accommodationist predecessors, the priests and kings who predated him, had bent over backward to assimilate, to let their invaders know that nothing was sacred. To convey that the concepts of only one God, the necessity of circumcision, and the avoidance of idol worship were mere preferences and not spiritual commands, Herod commanded the placement of a golden eagle in front of the massive Jewish temple in a nod to Greek mythology—the eagle signified the mythical god Jupiter. It was reminiscent of those Jewish men who decades before decided to remove the marks of their circumcision (1 Corinthians 7:18) so that in the gyms and dressing areas they would not look appreciably different from their non-Jewish counterparts.

In Herod's Rome, we have a police state with stunning brutality in service of a government with a primary aim to destroy a people and obliterate their culture and faith traditions. We have an oppressed people whose leaders decided to compromise rather than stand on principle. We have an ethno-cultural–religious group willing to engage in self-harm just to fit in. It is a perfect recipe for trauma.

"Traumatic experiences can impact an individual's health and well-being. However, traumatic experiences also may be collectively experienced, affecting a broader scope of individuals," wrote author Lauren Weisner in "Individual and Community Trauma: Individual Experiences in Collective Environments."[3]

When a group of people are mistreated, brutalized, and stripped of their cultural and oral history simply because of who they are and how they can be exploited, that is a form of collective trauma. This is the milieu into which our "meek," "submissive" Mary enters. Does it sound familiar?

In that environment, with a level of hate and oppression that was palpable, and constant, and most of all visible to everyone, she voiced her agreement with an angel of God to bring a child into this very difficult world—a child who was born the Savior, and who would change the world as it was known then.

We would like to present to you a more contemporary set of women who did the same thing—with results that were also world-changing. After all, whenever we as women choose to bring a child into the world, we are tacitly agreeing with God that this life has worth and value and that, regardless of our circumstances, we agree at the very least to give birth. But the women we are about to introduce to you went beyond that. They raised children who made us think and who grew to wrest change out of a system thousands of miles away from where from Jesus was born and nearly two millennia later. "May your word to me be fulfilled," said Mary to the angel Gabriel (Luke 1:38). These next three women echoed that sentiment when they gave birth to three men who had enormous impact on the world.

Let us say their names: Alberta Williams King. Emma Berdis Jones Baldwin. Louise Langdon Norton Little. The mothers of change agents Rev. Dr. Martin Luther King, James Baldwin, and Malcolm Little, who became Malcolm X. Their similarities to Mary, if you examine each of their lives closely, are stunning.

These women were born at about the same time, between roughly 1894 and 1904, and each of their respective man-children came into the world in the decade leading up to the Great Depression: James Baldwin in 1924, Malcolm X in 1925, and King in 1929.

> **Let us say their names: Alberta Williams King. Emma Berdis Jones Baldwin. Louise Langdon Norton Little.**

Sadly, like Mary, each of these mothers were alive to see their children die—two from violence to the body and one, perhaps, from violence to the soul.

For the descriptions of these women, we are deeply indebted to this reference: *The Three Mothers: How the Mothers of Martin Luther King, Jr., Malcolm X, and James Baldwin Shaped a Nation* by Anna Malaika Tubbs.

Louise

Louise Little was Louise Langdon at birth on the small Windward island of Grenada. This is a country that was invaded by the French in the fifteenth century, where dozens of Grenadians jumped from a hill overlooking the Caribbean Sea. They chose death over surrendering.[4] Grenada was part of the Transatlantic Slave Trade—a place where European colonizers stole land and set up plantations, then stole African people to work those plantations. Just as in America, these African people were constantly fighting for their physical freedom and spiritual dignity. The touchstone for this ongoing fight was Fedon's Rebellion; while halted by the British rulers, this was one of the first major volleys that ultimately led to Grenada's independence.

Louise was part of that revolutionary tradition, with grandparents who taught Louise about her African heritage and recounted the liberation stories of her Grenadian history. Their love and their stories were a welcome, comforting, and freeing antidote to the narrative the colonizers tried to indoctrinate her and other people of color on the island with—a familiar narrative of Black inferiority and the natural order of White rulership. Louise was born into a family of some means, where the men and women had skills they could trade for shelter, food, and a few more creature comforts. She learned poetry, was multilingual, and she loved words.[5]

She later became a follower of Marcus Garvey, who preached Black freedom and economic independence as he also advocated that Black Americans make their home on the African continent, away from the deep oppression that characterized the United States at the beginning of the twentieth century. It is important to note that Garvey's roots were in the church—first the Roman Catholic Church and later the African Orthodox Church. He made frequent references to God and the Bible, saying that "God and Nature first made us what we are, and then out of our own created genius we make ourselves what we want to be," and quoting often Psalm 68:31, "Princes shall come out of Egypt; Ethiopia shall soon stretch out her hands unto God."[6]

Berdis

Emma Berdis Jones was a writer who birthed one of the most important writers and thinkers of the twentieth century, James Baldwin. Her father had a skill—sailing—that gave him a level of freedom and protection as a merchant marine. The federal government conferred upon these "Black Jacks," as they were called, US citizenship not afforded to those of their color who were enslaved. She lost her mother as an infant. Like Louise, she loved writing and poetry as a young girl.

Berdis gave birth to her first child, James Baldwin, as a young unmarried woman. She met and married Rev. David Baldwin when James was a young boy. The dynamics of that marriage are well documented by Baldwin in his novels and autobiographical essays. Rev. Baldwin was a Pentecostal preacher who suffered from mental illness, and physically and emotionally abused his wife and eight children. Yet Berdis, who died in her nineties, years after her famous son died of cancer, shared great wisdom with James and his siblings. "Berdis reminded her children of the need to care for one another, to love one another, and to do the same for others outside of their home."[7] In fact, she insisted that James visit his stepfather as he was dying in a mental institution, for closure. She believed deeply in the power of love and forgiveness.

Alberta

Relative to Louise and Berdis, Alberta King (born Alberta Williams) enjoyed a measure of privilege. Her father was pastor of the growing Ebenezer Baptist Church, the church her son Martin would eventually lead. Her parents were devoutly Christian and unapologetically involved in activism in the segregated South—a singular act of bravery that put their entire family's lives at risk every day. Alberta became an accomplished musician who used her skills to minister to the congregation on Sundays. Possessing more education than her husband, Michael, she tutored him, and eventually he would succeed his father-in-law as Ebenezer's pastor. The couple would continue to build on the activist roots of the church.

> Perhaps they were all passionate about different forms of art because of the opportunity it offered them for creation; the opportunity to picture and build more beyond what was presented to them.[8]

These are the women who raised arguably three of the most impactful individuals of the mid-twentieth century. The men they raised profoundly changed the world and courageously spoke truth to power.

Like Jesus did.

How does the world that these three women inhabited compare to the beginning of the first millennium AD?

That was a world where the gulf between rich and poor was vast. A Roman empire that spanned more than two million square miles. A client-state, Israel, led by kings who, as God predicted hundreds of years earlier, would oppress them and exact onerous tax burdens (1 Samuel 8:5–19).

Compare that to the 1920s—the decade all three of the famous sons were born. The top 5 percent of US citizens owned more than one-third of the wealth, and the majority of families lived below the poverty line.[9]

The nation of Israel existed in a world characterized by vicious and relentless oppression and terror based on ethnicity. By the beginning of the first millennium, they had been under foreign rule for hundreds of years—the Babylonians, the Persians, the Greeks, and others—and were then ruled by the Roman Empire. Israel was a nation that was birthed under the theological mantle of one God and no other (Exodus 20:3). They were to bow to no human being. During the reign of another nation, the Seleucids, in the second century BC, Israelites were actually forbidden to worship their God freely and, on pain of death, made to sacrifice to gods other than Yahweh. As a result, Israelites who maintained fidelity to Jewish law were incensed by their fellow Jews who decided to take the "safe route" and submit to their oppressor's demands.

The latter were the very first "Uncle Toms," if you will. They would find their counterparts more than sixteen hundred years later, when Africans were brought to these shores and would ultimately fight among themselves regarding how to deal with White supremacy and terroristic oppression. Should they go along to get along, as some Jewish people did under the Seleucids? Or should they fight back and refuse to submit to the oppressive, brutal system of slavery?

It was a world where the oppressed had grown tired and weary and therefore banded together in revolutionary groups to fight their oppressors. In response to these egregious insults, groups of Jewish resistors arose. Interestingly, it was the local priests and Israelites who lived outside of the urban areas—the agrarian Jews—who sparked this movement. A man by the name of Mattathias witnessed a fellow Jewish man sacrifice to a pagan god and killed him on the spot. The story is told in the apocryphal book of First Maccabees, and the tale of the successful revolt that defeated the Seleucids is still celebrated today by observant Jews all over the world. It is called Hanukkah: the Festival of Lights. This story finds many counterparts in our own African American history, including the preachers Nat Turner and Denmark Vesey, who were equally incensed by their enslavers' crimes against humanity and took similar action. In the twentieth century, we would find others who took to the streets in myriad ways, violent and nonviolent, to continue the fight for dignity and freedom.

Louise, Berdis, and Alberta were born into a time that almost mirrored the era of Jesus's mother. Their responses were similar as well.

Mary's Magnificat seems to be all but forgotten in the annals of biblical history. We are much more familiar with the verse in Luke 1:38: "I am the Lord's servant. . . . May your word to me be fulfilled." Mary said this to the angel Gabriel, who had just given her the startling news that she, a virgin, would become pregnant with the child Jesus, who would save His people—her people. She submitted to God's invitation and directive and seemed to do so easily. The Magnificat, Mary's song, tells us why.

As soon as Mary received the news that she was to have a child, Scripture tells us that she rushed to visit a relative—her cousin Elizabeth, a much older woman seemingly past childbearing age, who held in her womb the man who would pave the way for Jesus's message. That man would himself be something of a revolutionary who challenged both the Jewish religious collaborators and the Roman oppressors. His name would be John—John the Baptist.

These two women got together to encourage each other. What they said to each other was Spirit led.

Elizabeth

In a loud voice she exclaimed: "Blessed are you among women, and blessed is the child you will bear! But why am I so favored, that the mother of my Lord should come to me? As soon as the sound of your greeting reached my ears, the baby in my womb leaped for joy. Blessed is she who has believed that the Lord would fulfill his promises to her!" (Luke 1:42–45).

Mary's song in response is known as the Magnificat:

> My soul glorifies the Lord
>   and my spirit rejoices in God my Savior,
> for he has been mindful
>   of the humble state of his servant.
> From now on all generations will call me blessed,
>   for the Mighty One has done great things for
>   me—
>   holy is his name.
> His mercy extends to those who fear him,
>   from generation to generation.
> He has performed mighty deeds with his arm;
>   he has scattered those who are proud in their
>   inmost thoughts.
> He has brought down rulers from their thrones
>   but has lifted up the humble.
> He has filled the hungry with good things
>   but has sent the rich away empty.
> He has helped his servant Israel,
>   remembering to be merciful
> to Abraham and his descendants forever,
>   just as he promised our ancestors. (Luke
>   1:46–55)

Mary and Elizabeth were joined forever in their parallel destinies. They raised sons of generational impact who changed the world and whose names are still called today. These were women who were conversant with their own ethnic history as people of the Torah. They were cognizant of their oppressive circumstances and determined that God would vindicate their cause and make them victorious by bringing down oppressive rulers, sending the rich away empty, and filling those who were hungry because of the evil practices of the religious rulers, who Jesus would say later "tie up heavy, cumbersome loads and put them on other people's shoulders, but they themselves are not willing to lift a finger to move them" (Matthew 23:4).

They had also seen an abhorrent and appalling thing. About one hundred years after the victory of the Maccabees, Rome conquered Israel again and the Maccabean descendants led another revolt in response to the erection of an idolatrous image over the Jewish temple, which violated the sacred law. These rebels, two thousand Jewish revolutionaries, were crucified on wooden poles—nailed and left to hang there, which they sometimes did for days or weeks until they died from suffocation or exhaustion. It happened a few years before Jesus's birth.[10]

Echoes. In 1919, around the time that Berdis, Louise, and Alberta came of age and gave birth to their famous sons, the National Association for the Advancement of Colored People (NAACP) published *Thirty Years of Lynching in the United States, 1889–1919.* This book of horrors documented nearly three thousand lynchings in the southern United States. Just like in the Roman Empire, the White supremacist practice of this gruesome method of dying was meant to send a clear message to any who would dare challenge the status quo: *Don't.*

Given their upbringing and the consciousness of their parents and ancestors, Berdis, Alberta, and Louise certainly knew of this document. But they knew even more personally. Alberta's husband, Michael, was born into a sharecropping family in Georgia, where he was beaten by White men but also had witnessed the horror of a lynching of a Black man who was robbed of his money by a gang of White men. Berdis watched her husband slowly and painfully lose his mind over the indignities that he suffered as a Black man in New York City, and her son, as he wended his way through insults and taunts to become a prolific and impactful writer, suffering internally from the never-ending assaults to his manhood and abilities. Finally Louise and her family were threatened in Philadelphia by the KKK and in Omaha, Nebraska, by White supremacists. Her husband, Earl, was brutally murdered in Lansing, Michigan, where he was said to have been shoved under a streetcar by the Black Legion, a White supremacist terror organization, for his continued activism. Louise had to view and identify her husband's mangled and torn body in the hospital.

Thankfully for all of us, Mary and Elizabeth did not cower in front of the challenges to their humanity and their freedom. Neither did Berdis, Alberta, and Louise.

Yet they persisted. In light of their oppressive conditions, Berdis, Alberta, and Louise engaged in the fight of their lives. Just like Mary and Elizabeth, they said yes to the call to raise sons who would challenge evil. But they didn't just agree to have children. Well before their children were born, they were engaged in civil rights work and civil disobedience.

Alberta worked tirelessly in the church, alongside her parents, her father, Rev. Adam Daniel Williams, and mother, Jennie Celeste, who attended historically Black Spelman College when it was Spelman Seminary. Her father is described as "a visionary who believed the church had a responsibility to fight racial injustice and empower its members through services that could meet all their basic needs."[11] Louise, who came to the United States from Grenada, learned about the freedom struggle in Grenada and the Caribbean islands and worked with her husband, Earl, in the Marcus Garvey movement. Finally, Berdis drove into her children's collective consciousness the importance of one word: love.

Baldwin got the message and helped millions see what his mother shared with him many years before, including in his book *The Price of the Ticket*:

> Love does not begin and end the way we seem to
> think it does. Love is a battle, love is a war; love
> is a growing up.

Hatred, which could destroy so much, never failed to destroy the man who hated, and this was an immutable law.[12]

Berdis was not the only mother who poured into her son. In fact, Malcolm X wrote this to one of his brothers about his mother's, Louise's, influence: "My accomplishments are ours, and yours are mine, but all of our achievements are Mom's, for she was a most Faithful Servant of the Truth years ago."[13]

Tubbs tells us that Louise "tried to learn as many [words] as she possibly could."[14] When Malcolm X went to prison, he describes in his autobiography how he read the dictionary from *A* to *Z* to learn as many words as he could, like his mother.

Echoes of Mother Mary

Joseph my husband
Taught him to earn a living
Working willingly with his hands.
He built and carpentered with such love
Carefully choosing every piece
Fitting each one together to make a perfect whole.
The same way He built His church.
But I taught Him to pray.
"Whatever you do," I told Him,
make sure you end with these words:
Thy will be done. Thy will be done.
"I did that," I told Him, "with you."
At first, I asked God, "How could this be?"
But then: Thy will be done. Thy will be done.
"Whatever you do," I told Him,
Make sure you say this:
May your kingdom come. May your kingdom
come.
"I did that," I told Him, "with you."
When I visited cousin Elizabeth, who was carrying
Your cousin, John,
She prophesied to me.

And I to her.
I said:
"He has filled the hungry
With good things
But has sent the rich empty away.
He has kept all His promises to us."
That is what His kingdom is like,
I told Him.
It is for all those who know their own hunger.
Not for those who are well, but for those who are
sick.
Be their physician, I told Him.
Be their physician.
Fill them
With good things.
After He died,
John told me of the things He said in my absence.
I smiled
And pondered His words in my heart.
Hearing the distant echo
Of my own voice.
And I know that my words
Were not in vain.

A Cloud of Women play

Rev. Dr. Martin Luther King Jr. had a similar story about his mother in his autobiography.

She told me about slavery. She tried to explain the divided system of the South—the segregated schools, restaurants, theaters, housing; the white and colored signs on drinking fountains, waiting rooms, lavatories—as a social condition rather than a natural order. She made it clear that she opposed the system and that I must never allow it to make me feel inferior. Then she said the words that almost every Negro hears before he

can yet understand the injustice that makes them
necessary: "you are as good as anyone."[15]

Mother Mary. Louise. Berdis. Alberta. They said yes to God
and gave birth. They spoke against the evil of the status quo
despite efforts to silence them. Each recognized her son's greatness and encouraged him in his destiny. They suffered from the
trauma of a genocidal-level hatred for people of their ethnicity,
in very personal ways. They dreamt of liberation and educated
themselves in the social order as well as their faith, which was
core to their identities. They raised their children to have faith
in the God of the Old and New Testaments. And they certainly
feared for their safety (what mother wouldn't?).

Tragically each of these women saw both the beginning and the
ending of their sons' lives. Two of them—Martin and Malcolm—
to the violence of murder directly related to the transformational
work they were doing in the world. One of them—Baldwin—to the
violent ravages of the cancer that riddled his body and sapped his
vitality.

Yet they persisted. All three women continued to live, although
only two of them continued to thrive. Alberta ministered with
her husband until, ironically, her murder by a White supremacist in 1974. Berdis lived into her nineties. Louise, who fought
to keep her children after the brutal murder of her husband, was
punished for her insistence that the state treat her family with dignity. They committed her to a mental institution, where she was
kept for more than twenty years. She was released two years after
Malcolm X was released from prison. But she lived to the ripe
old age of ninety-seven, outliving her son by more than thirty-five
years.

I'd like to think that Alberta, Berdis, and Louise met up with
their predecessors Mary and Elizabeth in heaven. I'd love to eaves-
drop on *that* conversation.

THE TALE
OF TWO TAMARS

Tamar, Tamar / Rev. Dr. Renita Weems, Betty Jean Owens

About three months later Judah was told, "Your
daughter-in-law Tamar is guilty of prostitution,
and as a result she is now pregnant." Judah said,
"Bring her out and have her burned to death!"

GENESIS 38:24

Then Amnon said to Tamar, "Bring the food here into my
bedroom so I may eat from your hand." And Tamar took
the bread she had prepared and brought it to her brother
Amnon in his bedroom. But when she took it to him to eat,
he grabbed her and said, "Come to bed with me, my sister."

2 SAMUEL 13:10–11

You would think that, as the princess in the kingdom
of the great King David, I would be treated like royalty.
It wasn't like that. I was at the mercy of my brothers. I
rarely even saw my father. But I did notice him talking
sometimes to some invisible person he called El. I would
find out later this El had many names. I would find
later that I needed to call some of those names myself.

A Cloud of Women play

There are two very different women named Tamar in the Bible. One was Jewish; the other was from the tribe of the Canaanites. One spoke up for herself and challenged dominant male authority; the other did not. One exercised her sexual agency toward the end of continuing the family name by initiating an intimate encounter with the father of her deceased husband. The other Tamar had her sexual agency brutally stolen. Both, however, were deeply challenged by male patriarchy and privilege. Let's examine their stories.

Tamar I: Brash and Brave

The first Tamar, whose life is examined and described in Genesis 38, was a young Israelite who was given in marriage to the firstborn son of Jacob and progenitor to one of the twelve tribes of Israel, Judah. As one of the progenitors, Judah held a position of honor and privilege. The moral code of the time expected him to be duty bound to obey the Ten Commandments and the laws Moses promulgated to the new nation of Israel at God's behest. As was the case of nearly every prominent biblical character whose life is described in the Bible, that did not happen.

Judah arranged for his firstborn son, Er, to marry Tamar. Scripture says that Er was evil and God cut his life short. As the Hebrew law required, Tamar was given in marriage to Er's brother Onan, but he also did evil in God's sight and died.

All that was left for Tamar to do, based on the Hebrew law to which they all were bound, was to return to her father's home and wait for the third brother, Shelah, to grow up. Apparently the fact that he was much younger than Tamar was no problem; the point was that Tamar had to produce a male heir in the line of her first husband.

Judah, though, was afraid that God would take Shelah's life, too, if he married Tamar. So he kept Shelah from her. That was when Tamar decided to take matters into her own hands. Judah had become a widower with the death of his wife, Shua. Tamar disguised herself as a temple prostitute and found out where Judah would be. He was traveling to the area where his sheep were grazing to oversee their shearing, a primary source of income.

Temple prostitutes were women who offered their bodies for money in what was believed at the time by other nations to be a sacred sexual rite. Some of the Hebrews had bought into that notion as well. But that was not Tamar's motivation. Her intent was to bear a child in her husband's name even if she had to do that by having her father-in-law, Judah, impregnate her. Having a male heir was a sacred, solemn duty in the minds of the Hebrew people, and the idea that Judah would prevent that was cruel and unjust to Tamar. Women, just as a practical manner, genuinely needed a husband for their physical and economic protection.

Tamar met Judah in the village of Timnah:

> "How much will you pay to have sex with me?" Tamar asked.
>
> "I'll send you a young goat from my flock," Judah promised.
>
> "But what will you give me to guarantee that you will send the goat?" she asked.
>
> "What kind of guarantee do you want?" he replied.
>
> She answered, "Leave me your identification seal and its cord and the walking stick you are carrying." So Judah gave them to her. Then he had intercourse with her, and she became pregnant. Afterward she went back home, took off her veil, and put on her widow's clothing as usual. (Genesis 38:16–19 NLT)

Judah still did not know who Tamar was. He sent his friend to the place where they had met to make the exchange and retrieve the guarantee he had given her of the walking stick and identification seal. When the friend could not find her, he asked the residents (only the men) where the shrine prostitute was.

"'There hasn't been any shrine prostitute here,' they said" (Genesis 38:21).

Judah, to avoid embarrassment, simply calls off the search and decides to call the guarantee items a loss.

Three months later the word got out in the community that Tamar was pregnant. Judah, still hiding from his sin, had this response: "Bring her out and have her burned to death!" (v. 38:24).

But Tamar had the guarantee items Judah had provided, and she used them to expose her father-in-law's hypocrisy.

Judah's response: "'She is more righteous than I, since I wouldn't give her to my son Shelah.' And he did not sleep with her again" (Genesis 38:26).

Judah's response sits in high contrast to some men today whose corruption is exposed for everyone to see, yet they categorically deny any wrongdoing. More than two thousand years ago, Tamar's response said to that insular Jewish community that if it is sin for an unmarried woman to get pregnant, it is just as much sin for the man who impregnated her.

Tamar's brave confrontation, as a woman in that era of even greater male dominance than now, is the precursor to Black women like Sojourner Truth. She so eloquently demanded justice for Black women and spoke for all women when she reminded her audience of the biological origin of Jesus the Christ.

Sojourner Truth delivered this speech in 1851 at the Women's Rights Convention in Akron, Ohio:

Ain't I a Woman?

Well, children, where there is so much racket there must be something out of kilter. I think that 'twixt the negroes of the South and the women at the North, all talking about rights, the white men will be in a fix pretty soon. But what's all this here talking about?

That man over there says that women need to be helped into carriages, and lifted over ditches, and to have the best place everywhere. Nobody ever helps me into carriages, or over mud-puddles, or gives me any best place! And ain't I a woman? Look at me! Look at my arm! I have ploughed and planted, and gathered into barns, and no man could head me! And ain't I a woman? I could work as much and eat as much as a man—when I could get it—and bear the lash as well! And ain't I a woman? I have borne thirteen children, and seen most all sold off to slavery, and when I cried out with my mother's grief, none but Jesus heard me! And ain't I a woman?

Then they talk about this thing in the head; what's this they call it? [member of audience whispers, "intellect"] That's it, honey. What's that got to do with women's rights or negroes' rights? If my cup won't hold but a pint, and yours holds a quart, wouldn't you be mean not to let me have my little half measure full?

Then that little man in black there, he says women can't have as much rights as men, 'cause Christ wasn't a woman! Where did your Christ come from? Where did your Christ come from? From God and a woman! Man had nothing to do with Him.

If the first woman God ever made was strong enough to turn the world upside down all alone, these women together ought to be able to turn it back, and get it right side up again! And now they is asking to do it, the men better let them.[1]

Tamar confronted sexism. Sojourner Truth confronted sexism. We have a third woman in our pantheon who was an unlikely advocate for gender equality. Her name was Rosa Parks.

We often think of Mrs. Parks as the mother of the civil rights movement, but there is an obscure story of her confronting Pope John Paul II in 1999:

> In the years since the Movement, Mrs. Parks has spoken publicly about the dangers of sexism. When she met Pope John Paul II in St. Louis, Mo., in 1999, she shared these words with the pontiff: "My lifetime mission has been simple— that all men and women are created equal under the eyes of our Lord." In the spirit of her activist mantra, "quiet strength," this simple sentence was Mrs. Parks's way of challenging women's secondary status in the Catholic Church.[2]

In fact, the civil rights movement was a place where Black women in particular were treated as second-class citizens. The idea that men should be dominant in all things has permeated the culture for millennia. Sadly, that idea was no less a governing principle even in a movement that celebrated human equality and freedom. Black women fought that battle within the movement for years without much recognition from the wider public.

And sexism has been a thorny issue in the church, including within the traditional Black church, for many years. Scholar and thought leader in this area Rev. Dr. Renita Weems confronts the reality of male hypocrisy as Tamar did. Weems's book *Battered Love* is a troubling and searing critique of the unchecked abuse that takes place in the church.

All men and women are created equal under the eyes of our Lord.
—Rosa Parks

Dr. Weems was raised in the Pentecostal tradition, with many of the historic strictures and restrictions on the role of women in the church. Through a complex maze of educational experiences, spiritual confrontations, and personal reflections, she developed an intriguing theory that became a seminal treatise about domestic and institutional violence against women. *Battered Love* draws an intriguing parallel between the "terrifying texts" in the Old Testament that use sexual and physical violence against women and the ongoing specter of abuse against women, including the abuse that takes place in churches:

> The prophets of Israel went to extraordinary lengths to convey to their audiences the nature, extent, and consequences of their actions. The prophets repeatedly called upon some of the most explicit, provocative, and lurid images of human sexuality to personify what they saw as the nation's religious distortions and political blunders. Unforgettable scenes of the rape, abuse, and mutilation of women are detailed to symbolize what in the prophets' thinking was the disgraceful fate that awaited the nation.[3]

Dr. Weems goes on to recount the biblical stories depicted in the books of Hosea and Jeremiah about "wayward" women who paid dire consequences for their actions in the form of abuse by other lovers and violent attacks on their bodies. These prophets, asserts Weems, were using these lurid, emotionally gripping images to arrest the attention of those Israeli leaders who were heaping oppression on their people and worshipping other gods. She posits the idea that humans being what they are, men misapplied these metaphors to develop a culture of permissiveness around the abuse of women itself, completely ignoring that these stories were merely tools to get to a deeper truth about the depth of God's frustration with the sin of His children. These poetically framed stories, she says, "were intended to cast Israel's behavior in the strongest moral terms possible" so that those who were violating God's covenant would be shamed into repentance.[4]

But with human beings, there are always unintended consequences.

Weems writes, "A risky metaphor gives rise to a risky deduction: in this case, to the extent that God's covenant with Israel is like a marriage between a man and a woman, and to the extent that divine retribution is theologically acceptable, the image of a husband physically retaliating against his wife becomes unavoidable. Such is the risk of metaphorical language."[5]

The antidote, Weems believes, is not to focus on the metaphor itself but instead on the point of the metaphorical story: that God's heart is broken when His children depart from the elements of their covenant with Him. When they mistreat and cheat each other, when they follow gods of wood and stone, when they ignore His guidance, the mighty God who made the universe is grieved to the core of His being. That is the point.

Weems is just one of many contemporary examples of women who, like Tamar, use their ingenuity to make a point about the hypocrisy of men who call themselves godly, or are even called godly by God himself, but act in a manner contrary to their calling.

Jesus reserved his harshest critique for the hypocrites of His day:

> Woe to you, teachers of the law and Pharisees, you hypocrites! You give a tenth of your spices—mint, dill and cumin. But you have neglected the more important matters of the law—justice, mercy and faithfulness. You should have practiced the latter, without neglecting the former. You blind guides! You strain out a gnat but swallow a camel.
>
> Woe to you, teachers of the law and Pharisees, you hypocrites! You clean the outside of the cup and dish, but inside they are full of greed and self-indulgence. Blind Pharisee! First clean the inside of the cup and dish, and then the outside also will be clean.
>
> Woe to you, teachers of the law and Pharisees, you hypocrites! You are like whitewashed tombs, which look beautiful on the outside but on the inside are full of the bones of the dead and everything unclean. In the same way, on the outside

you appear to people as righteous but on the inside you are full of hypocrisy and wickedness.

Woe to you, teachers of the law and Pharisees,
you hypocrites! You build tombs for the prophets
and decorate the graves of the righteous. And you
say, "If we had lived in the days of our ancestors,
we would not have taken part with them in shedding the blood of the prophets." So you testify
against yourselves that you are the descendants
of those who murdered the prophets. Go ahead,
then, and complete what your ancestors started!

You snakes! You brood of vipers! How will
you escape being condemned to hell? (Matthew
23:23–33)

These women—Tamar, Sojourner, and now Dr. Renita Weems—
stand in the best tradition of God himself. They revealed what was
already there and worked, and are now working, to change what
is for what can be. They deserve our respect and honor.

Tamar II: The Acted Upon

Clearly, the first Tamar was a bold and courageous woman. She
took a big risk and brought to his knees one of the pillars of
Israel, at the possible cost of her own life. There was, however,
a second Tamar. Her story is the opposite of Judah's daughter-
in-law.

"In the course of time, Amnon son of David fell in love with
Tamar, the beautiful sister of Absalom son of David" (2 Samuel
13:1).

Take a look. Amnon is the son of David, and Tamar is a daughter of David. Same father, different mothers. And *love* was not the
right word here. In fact, the writer defines what the situation was
in the very next verse: "Amnon became so obsessed with his sister
Tamar that he made himself ill. She was a virgin, and it seemed
impossible for him to do anything to her" (v. 2).

Amnon couldn't do anything *to* her. He was not interested in connecting on any level. He wanted control. The events in the biblical account in 2 Samuel 13 proceed from that. We read in these verses that, on the counsel of his cousin, who held the title of adviser and is described as shrewd, Amnon feigned illness and asked his father, David, to have Tamar bring food to him. It was, of course, a ruse.

Tamar obeyed. After all, her dad was the king! And why would she not exercise kindness to help her family? She made bread for him right in his house, which was away from the king's palace and away, presumably, from the king's prying eyes. There was a reason for that.

Amnon did not immediately take the bread from Tamar's hand.

> "Send everyone out of here," Amnon said. So everyone left him. Then Amnon said to Tamar, "Bring the food here into my bedroom so I may eat from your hand." And Tamar took the bread she had prepared and brought it to her brother Amnon in his bedroom. But when she took it to him to eat, he grabbed her and said, "Come to bed with me, my sister." (2 Samuel 13:9–11)

Tamar's first instinct was to refuse him, which she did assertively and with strength.

> "No, my brother!" she said to him. "Don't force me! Such a thing should not be done in Israel! Don't do this wicked thing. What about me? Where could I get rid of my disgrace? And what about you? You would be like one of the wicked fools in Israel." (vv. 12–13)

She must have been afraid. But she was not paralyzed. She was quick-witted and even made what was certainly a fake claim:

"Please speak to the king; he will not keep me from being married to you" (v. 13).

The time when half-siblings could marry and have children had been over since Moses gave the laws to the children of Israel. The only recorded half-sibling marriage in the Bible was between Abraham and Sarah. I would posit that Tamar was simply buying time to avoid the unthinkable.

This next verse proves what we instinctively know: rape is not passion, or love, or lust—it is the desire to consume, to control. "But he refused to listen to her, and since he was stronger than she, he raped her" (v. 14).

What's love got to do with it? Nothing.

> Then Amnon hated her with intense hatred. In fact, he hated her more than he had loved her. Amnon said to her, "Get up and get out!"
>
> "No!" she said to him. "Sending me away would be a greater wrong than what you have already done to me."
>
> But he refused to listen to her. (vv. 15–16)

The dysfunction of the times is on full display. As a woman who was no longer a virgin, Tamar was now "damaged goods" to her community. Any possible suitors would be put off. Victim or not, she would be shamed and shunned. In Israel there was no use for a single woman, never married, without children.

> He called his personal servant and said, "Get this woman out of my sight and bolt the door after her." So his servant put her out and bolted the door after her. She was wearing an ornate robe, for this was the kind of garment the virgin daughters of the king wore. Tamar put ashes on her head and tore the ornate robe she was wearing. She put her hands on her head and went away, weeping aloud as she went. (vv. 17–19)

In the space of probably less than an hour, Tamar went from princess to pariah. Like many women today, she is urged by Absalom, her own brother, not to tell.

> Her brother Absalom said to her, "Has that Amnon, your brother, been with you? Be quiet for now, my sister; he is your brother. Don't take this thing to heart." And Tamar lived in her brother Absalom's house, a desolate woman. (v. 20)

This unthinkable thing that happened to Tamar more than two thousand years ago happens about every sixty-eight seconds in the United States, according to RAINN (Rape, Abuse & Incest National Network), and one in six women in our country have been sexually assaulted.[6] Women who were victims were told, like Tamar, to stay quiet and get over it. They lived lives of desolation, always in the shadow and memory of the trauma that happened. Until the #MeToo Movement, which broke open the stench and extent of these abuses at the highest levels of business and government. Thank God for the movement that turned the spotlight on the men and is beginning to let them know they will pay their own consequences for their cruel and brutal acts.

The first Tamar, victim of her father-in-law who refused to allow her access to womanhood, which was defined at the time as motherhood, took action. The second Tamar, the victim of a heinous crime and paralyzed by pain and trauma, retreated to her brother's house, "weeping aloud as she went" (v. 19).

In 2010, author Danielle L. McGuire released *At the Dark End of the Street: Black Women, Rape, and Resistance—a New History of the Civil Rights Movement from Rosa Parks to the Rise of Black Power*. It conveys a vital message about the power dynamic of rape, and the previously untold story of Rosa Park's involvement in this issue as well. This power dynamic has plagued sinful human beings since the beginning of time. We see it with Amnon, who used his individual power to take what he wanted regardless of the feelings of his victim. But we also see it in the ancient nations, including the nation of Israel. This is what our beloved Moses tells Israel to do when it conquers the cities of Canaan:

> When the LORD your God delivers it into your hand, put to the sword all the men in it. As for the women, the children, the livestock and everything else in the city, you may take these as plunder for yourselves. And you may use the plunder the LORD your God gives you from your enemies. (Deuteronomy 20:13–14)

Rape is a universal tool used to solidify power individually as well as nationally and systemically. In the United States it was used by White men to send a message to Black men and women that they, as a group, were not in control of anything pertaining to their own survival. Rapes and gang rapes were so common in the South that more than a decade before her refusal to yield her bus seat to a White man launched the Civil Rights Movement, the activist Rosa Parks investigated the brutal gang rape of Betty Jean Owens, a Florida A&M University (FAMU) coed traveling back from a school dance with her friends in Tallahassee. Four White men made the two young Black male students leave. While the second woman escaped, Owens was forced into the men's car. The youngest male in the gang was sixteen years old. The assailants were apprehended, arrested, and jailed, pending trial.

FAMU students demonstrated en masse at the jail and at the trial and even led a boycott. (The year was 1944, eleven years before the famous Montgomery Bus Boycott.) McGuire reports that when Owens gave her testimony, she refused to answer when the defense attorney asked whether she was a virgin.[7] The medical report and eyewitness accounts of her friends, in the end, led to the very first guilty verdict against White men accused of raping a Black woman.

Rape against women is a horrific exercise of brute male power. Rape against African American women is a way to ensure that an entire race is silenced:

When African Americans tested their freedom during Reconstruction, former slaveholders and their sympathizers used rape as a "weapon of terror" to dominate the bodies and minds of African-American men and women.[8]

The cases of Tamar and Owens show the troubling and continuing specter of this horrific crime, the valiant efforts of women to resist being victimized in this way, and the brute force that refuses to yield. The hard callousness of the rapist, calcified and petrified around the heart, has meant trauma for millions of girls and women.

I want to reach across the ages and enfold Tamar in my arms. I want to rock her, and stroke her head, and tell her she was not at fault. I want to tell her to look at her past namesake to gather strength to confront a system of female subjugation that would deny her the ability to heal and to live a life of joy and freedom, a system that would tell her she is less than a woman because of a hateful man's action, and that would demand she retreat and accept her fate.

The two Tamars. One took her sexuality into her own hands toward a cultural and—even Judah admits—noble end. The other had her sexuality brutally ripped from her against her will. Both confronted male dominance. But the one who was able to exercise agency and effectively confront the hypocrisy won in the end.

We honor the two Tamars, the one who acted and the one who was acted upon, the one who confronted hypocrisy and won and the one who tried to stop evil but was overwhelmed. We honor yesterday's and today's Tamars in both categories, including Betty Jean Owens. We find strength in knowing that our stories are not unique but part of a cloud of women's stories, and the women in that cloud are urging us: Don't quit. Don't give up. Fight. Heal. I was you once.

SAVING BLACK BOYS

Shiphrah, Puah / Marian Wright Edelman

The king of Egypt said to the Hebrew midwives, whose names were Shiphrah and Puah, "When you are helping the Hebrew women during childbirth on the delivery stool, if you see that the baby is a boy, kill him; but if it is a girl, let her live." The midwives, however, feared God and did not do what the king of Egypt had told them to do; they let the boys live.

EXODUS 1:15–17

SHIPHRAH

I was angry at Pharaoh. He compelled us to labor. And conspired to kill our sons, the joy of their fathers.

PUAH

We knew what he wanted to do. He was trying to exterminate a nation, a nation of God's own inheritance. He was trying to keep the deliverer from coming.

SHIPHRAH

Pharaoh didn't know that God himself was our deliverer.

PUAH

How could we kill our seed? We wouldn't dare touch these loved ones of God.

A Cloud of Women play

They were splendid and beautiful. The women Shiphrah ("splendid") and Puah ("beautiful") lived in a brutal time. A time when a wicked ruler was afraid of an entire people. Not because of what they were doing to him, but because of what he was doing to them.

> Now Joseph and all his brothers and all that generation died, but the Israelites were exceedingly fruitful; they multiplied greatly, increased in numbers and became so numerous that the land was filled with them. (Exodus 1:6–7)

The book of Genesis recounts how Joseph became the reason that the chosen people of God went en masse to Egypt. He is the one who was despised by his brothers and left for dead, then sold by them to nomadic traders who bartered his body for the material goods they desired (37:1–36). When the land of his father and brothers and their wives and progeny fell into drought and famine, they decided that Egypt, brimming with grain and spice, would be a good place to go. It was a rich country with an even richer heritage. Their brother Joseph had positioned himself—rather, God had positioned him—to become the second-highest government official in the land.

In all, seventy of Joseph's family came to Egypt. The account in Genesis describes how these men, women, and children came to be enslaved. The famine that drove Joseph's family to Egypt eventually spread to Egypt herself, and all those in the land agreed to sell themselves to Pharaoh just so they could survive. (See Genesis 47:13–20.)

The survival instinct is irrepressible. Most people will do anything to keep from dying.

This story in Exodus helps us to see how the children of Israel—the name God gave to Joseph's father, Jacob, when he survived a wrestling match with Him—were blessed with fruitfulness, so much so that their numbers exceeded the population of original Egyptians.

The pharaoh of Egypt was not pleased. We are not told

why—after all, everyone who lived in Egypt was already living on land owned by Pharaoh, and they all had to give him one-fifth of everything the land yielded. Pharaoh was rich and fat. Why did he want more?

> Then a new king, to whom Joseph meant nothing, came to power in Egypt. "Look," he said to his people, "the Israelites have become far too numerous for us. Come, we must deal shrewdly with them or they will become even more numerous and, if war breaks out, will join our enemies, fight against us and leave the country." (Exodus 1:8–10)

Pharaoh was talking to *his* people. That's human nature too. We stratify and classify people. It didn't matter how long the family of Jacob (Israel) had been there—they were still *othered* by the king. People who are othered are thought not to be trusted. *They might do something to me. They're different. They worship differently and think differently. I don't understand them.*

So the king had an idea. An awful idea.

> So they put slave masters over them to oppress them with forced labor, and they built Pithom and Rameses as store cities for Pharaoh. But the more they were oppressed, the more they multiplied and spread; so the Egyptians came to dread the Israelites and worked them ruthlessly. They made their lives bitter with harsh labor in brick and mortar and with all kinds of work in the fields; in all their harsh labor the Egyptians worked them ruthlessly. (vv. 11–14)

To Pharaoh's chagrin, the affliction did not have its desired effect. As comedian Robin Harris famously said: "We don't die, we multiply."[1]

We don't know exactly how Pharaoh and his people were able to subjugate the Israelites, who were more numerous than the entire Egyptian population. Military might? Maybe the Israelites passed down the story of how the previous Pharaoh was so kind to their ancestor Joseph and they owed a debt to the Egyptians for saving their lives. Maybe the Egyptians told that story to them too.

We don't know, either, why the Egyptians were so afraid of their subjects. Was it their numbers? Was it their own guilt at how they were treating these people who had done nothing to them? Or was it just that they were *different*?

The more they multiplied, the greater the Egyptian fear, until it metastasized into a murderous rage.

Enter the two Hebrew midwives. Their legacy is explained so quickly—tucked in the folds between the long narrative about Joseph and his slow but brilliant rise to power at the end of Genesis, and the fabulous story of Moses leading the Israelites to freedom that dominates the first part of Exodus—that we can easily breeze by it with barely a passing glance. After all, midwives are servants, not government leaders or freedom fighters. They live routine, repetitive lives without much fanfare.

But the life of a midwife is glorious; she has the great honor to coach a mother bringing a new life into the world. She soothes her and eases her pain. Reassures her that all will be well. Grieves with her when that new life does not come to be. Helps a mother honor a life gone too soon, right at the moment it happens. These splendid, beautiful women, Shiphrah and Puah, did that every day. They surely had learned over the years the best methods for delivering breech babies, and easing the mother's nausea, and severing the cord tying mother to newly minted human. They rejoiced with her, held her hand, spoke life to her, and cleaned and held the baby even before the mother. I am sure Shiphrah and Puah did this. Because they feared God. "The fear of the LORD is a fountain of life" (Proverbs 14:27). Does this ever describe Shiphrah and Puah, who had brought life to all those Hebrew babies born into a regime of oppression and fear and brutality! Imagine their horror when this happened:

> The king of Egypt said to the Hebrew midwives,
> whose names were Shiphrah and Puah, "When
> you are helping the Hebrew women during
> childbirth on the delivery stool, if you see that
> the baby is a boy, kill him; but if it is a girl, let
> her live." (Exodus 1:15–16)

Pharaoh had it out especially for the sons. Boy infants turn
into men, and don't all men like power? The one holding the
power certainly thought so. Pharaoh was desperate to hold on
to what he had, so much so that he assumed all men would be
like him. He was threatened by the male gender of these fruitful,
multiplying people. Their men would be his downfall.

Ironic, isn't it, that those who claim the most power also have
the most fear?

But the midwives revered God and human life. The midwives hated evil. "To fear the LORD is to hate evil" (Proverbs
8:13). After years of wresting life out of mothers' bodies, years
of rejoicing and consoling, years of holding precious new life,
how could they possibly do what the king was telling them
to do? Their very bodies and spirits must have recoiled at the
thought.

"The fear of the LORD is the beginning of wisdom" (Proverbs
9:10). *No*, they said to themselves. *No.* But how would they tell
Pharaoh that?

The midwives feared God more than they feared the king of
Egypt. Despite Pharaoh's command, they kept the male children
alive.

> The king of Egypt summoned the midwives and
> asked them, "Why have you done this? Why
> have you let the boys live?"
> The midwives answered Pharaoh, "Hebrew
> women are not like Egyptian women; they are
> vigorous and give birth before the midwives ar-
> rive." (Exodus 1:18–19)

Shiphrah and Puah decided they would not tell the king of their plans. They simply went back to what they knew best: delivering babies. Fearlessly ignoring the potential consequences, which could have been certain death. *There are more of us*, they might have thought. *They can't kill us all.*

Interesting. The king did not chastise these brave servant women, who were double servants: they served their own people as well as the king. And they hid from the king their real motivation for saving the male children—in fact, they lied. They feared God, and they lied. Isn't that a contradiction? Artist Marvin Gaye's groundbreaking album of 1971, *What's Going On?*, answers that question in his passionate song "Save the Children." He urges us to live for the children.

Save the children. Whatever the cost.

Save the children. Whatever the cost.

There is a long tradition in the faith community of practicing civil disobedience, which is the refusal to obey the political authorities, to make a political statement, or to achieve a political end. That practice is illustrated in the person of Jesus Christ, who intentionally healed many on the Sabbath, over religious leaders' stern objections that it was a violation of the commandment not to work on the Sabbath, with *healing* defined by them as work (see Matthew 12:10; Mark 3:2; Luke 13:10–13; John 7:23). He clearly had violated the authorities as He sought and heeded a higher Authority. Jesus was making a point, illustrating the wise observation that God is always working, and He was shining a light on the spiritual value of demonstrated compassion for another's suffering. The midwives are firmly in the line of that noble service.

Marian Wright Edelman

Children's advocate Marian Wright Edelman, Founder and President Emerita of the Children's Defense Fund, has a similar pedigree. Like the Hebrew midwives Shiphrah and Puah, she was raised in a community marked by faith. "Daddy was the preacher and teacher and Mama the church organizer and fundraiser," she explains in her book *The Measure of Our Success: A Letter to My Children and Yours*.[2] Her father was a Baptist minister who poured into her until his untimely death when she was only fourteen years old. Her parents' lessons imprinted empathy and other principles on her mind and spirit, and she has lived them out, and is living them out, in ways we can only call remarkable.

> We were told that the world had a lot of problems; that Black people had an extra lot of problems, but that we were able and obligated to struggle and change them . . . and that extra intellectual and material gifts brought with them the privilege and responsibility of sharing with others less fortunate. . . . Service . . . is the very purpose of life and not something you do in your spare time.[3]

And so struggle she did.

Isn't it interesting that the stories in the Bible of mass killings perpetrated by Israel's enemies targeted the male children? It happened in the days of Moses and triggered a mass exodus from Egypt by the Hebrew people, directed by God into their land of promise. It happened around the time of Jesus's birth, prompting Mary and Joseph to flee with Him to Africa—specifically Egypt, where His ancestors had fled from hundreds of years before—and hide out until the danger was past. Imagine a king's mad lust for power that would cause him to make such a cruel and inhuman decree. Imagine Shiphrah and Puah tending with loving care to these Hebrew mothers and their brown babies. Imagine their horror at the very idea that they would do anything to these babies but usher them safely out of the womb and into the world—albeit a world, in their sphere, that already hated them and wanted them dead.

It is in their courageous spirit that Marian Wright Edelman has continued to work and advocate. Her parents sent her off to historically Black Spelman College, where she learned and bonded with other Black women and gained knowledge and wisdom for her journey. She finished Yale Law School and turned right back around to the South, to Mississippi, calling it "the worst symbol of the segregated prison that the South represented then."[4] There she worked for the NAACP Legal Defense and Education Fund, where she defended advocates for voting rights during Mississippi Freedom Summer in 1964.

Those efforts in the mid- and late 1960s were successful by anyone's standards. The Civil Rights Act was passed in 1964, opening up public accommodations to all people regardless of race or ethnicity. The Voting Rights Act was signed in 1965 by President Lyndon Baines Johnson, obliterating some of the egregious practices that local governments used to keep Black folks from exercising their right to vote for the candidate of their choice—with Rev. Martin Luther King standing behind President Johnson at the signing ceremony along with many other civil rights leaders.

Marian Wright Edelman, the attorney, was gratified at these wins. While she realized those wins were necessary, she knew they were insufficient to create the kind of change she, her colleagues, and fellow activists sought. In fact, that activism came at a price: "The cost of that for many was that they got kicked off the plantations and lost that little bit of money, unjust as it was, that they had had to survive."[5] And so Edelman, along with others, did what Shiphrah and Puah did. Kind of. In 1967, Marian went to the "king"—in this case, Congress—and spoke to them directly.

"I wish the senators would have a chance to go and just look at the empty cupboards in the Delta and the number of people who are going around and begging just to feed their children," Edelman said.[6] This is the testimony she gave:

> I ended up touring the Delta of Mississippi with Bobby Kennedy because he came down as a substitute for Teddy Kennedy when Joe

Clark's senate committee on labor and education came to Mississippi. We had been having enormous numbers of Head Start battles, and I had gone up to testify before the committee in Washington about the growing hunger in Mississippi and the fact that many Blacks were being pushed off the plantations. And I told the committee, please come and see yourselves. Because they didn't quite believe me when I talked about how the conditions of life, the poverty was getting worse, and the people really didn't have enough to eat in Mississippi. And so they came, and Bobby Kennedy came with them. And while they were there to examine the impact of the poverty program on Mississippi Blacks and Whites, I used it as an opportunity to tell them about growing hunger in the Delta, and they were shocked. And happily one or two of the senators agreed to stay over and to go up on the Delta to see for themselves if—whether it was true that people were starving. And so Bobby Kennedy agreed to be one of those senators, and happily he went. And he saw, and he made hunger an issue.[7]

It would be an understatement to say that the experience was eye opening for Senator Robert Kennedy Jr. As he walked through the Mississippi Delta, he was stunned. As he visited a shack that housed a family that included seven children, he said, "My God, I didn't know this kind of thing existed. How can a country like this allow it? Maybe they just don't know."[8]

Sadly, some did know. But Kennedy returned to Washington, and his colleague Joseph P. Clark pulled together a set of hearings to bring public attention to the reality of mass starvation in Mississippi—the result of Black people being kicked off the plantations when the work picking cotton disappeared, along with racist-driven pushback from southern senators who resisted the federal government's efforts to alleviate poverty.

The public pressure and the embarrassment of even the most racist politicians led Congress to pass a $10 million emergency fund for food and medical services. Soon after, Senator Robert Kennedy, on hearing from Edelman that she was going to visit Dr. King, urged her to "tell Dr. King to bring the poor people to Washington."[9] That's what prompted King to launch the Poor People's Campaign.

As Edelman pushed forward, she came into her passion: saving the children. The twin murders of Dr. King and Robert Kennedy were dagger blows to the heart of the Civil Rights Movement and to those who were deeply engaged, as Edelman was.

Yet she persisted. Edelman was part of the founding of Head Start, a program launched in 1965 that provides free preschool to children from low-income families. In the 1970s she fully embraced her mission to children and founded the Children's Defense Fund, an institution that lives today—a testament to her strong conviction that prevention and preparation programming for children would make a major difference in our nation's ability to thrive and prosper. In the 1990s she mobilized two hundred thousand people to come to Washington, DC, to protest the welfare reform bill that President Bill Clinton signed into law, asserting that it would ultimately hurt children the most.

The Hebrew midwives faced a major challenge, seemingly insurmountable: What would they do about Pharaoh? They strategized, making the decision that the only way out of obeying his edict would be to lie. Save the babies' lives one at a time . . . and lie about why they were still living, despite the demands of their government. They refused to throw their hands up in despair. They pushed through, knowing their very lives were on the line.

Marian Wright Edelman did the same. She put her life on the line, first for Black voting rights, then for poor people, and finally for children. The only difference was in her tactics. Instead of being forced to lie, she was compelled to tell the truth about the condition of her fellow human beings. Thankfully for all of us, the truth worked to break hard hearts and alter the way the United States would deal with poverty and discrimination.

When I look at photos of Marian Wright Edelman or see her interviewed on television, what strikes me most is the calmness in her countenance and her voice. She is clearly a woman at peace with herself. How does such a fighter, who is always seemingly climbing uphill against unbelievable odds, appear to be so peaceful? The Washington University interview gives a hint at her secret. There is a segment where she talks about her community—parents, church, extended family, and friends: "They never cracked a book of theology or philosophy, but the thing that they anchored us in was that the kingdom of God is within."[10]

Genesis tells us that the Hebrew midwives feared God rather than Pharaoh. They refused to bow, and they figured out how to "make a way out of no way," as the older saints say. They stubbornly refused to give up. Like Marian. "Giving up was simply not a part of the language of my childhood or my upraising. You don't give up. Nobody has a right to give up on any child."[11]

> The fear of the LORD leads to life;
> then one rests content, untouched by trouble.
> (Proverbs 19:23)

RAISING THE DEAD

Rizpah / Sybrina Fulton, Ida B. Wells-Barnett

He handed them over to the Gibeonites, who killed them
and exposed their bodies on a hill before the LORD. All seven
of them fell together; they were put to death during the first
days of the harvest, just as the barley harvest was beginning.

Rizpah daughter of Aiah took sackcloth and
spread it out for herself on a rock. From the beginning of the harvest till the rain poured down from
the heavens on the bodies, she did not let the birds
touch them by day or the wild animals by night.

2 SAMUEL 21:9–10

To have your loved ones die without a proper
burial was an unthinkable shame.

A Cloud of Women play

She refused. They had already been murdered. She refused to
let the memory of their lives be murdered as well. They were
her sons, and they were men. Full grown, complicated, filled with
the potential of their future, they had been snuffed out by blood
violence, like the flickering of warm, bright candles suddenly
blown out.

It was not her sons' fight—their execution arose out of the
broken promise of the previous generation. It had to do with a

slaughter in which they played no part, and yet their lives were taken under the authority of King David, an authority no one challenged—a power conflict as old as time between their father, Saul, and the Gibeonites. Saul, in his rage and in his pride, broke the agreement between Joshua and Gibeon and killed many Gibeonites. Now the Gibeonite descendants wanted revenge.

And don't we still? Still want revenge for shed blood and offended pride, for liberties taken and liberties stolen, for violence to body and soul?

The Gibeonites wanted blood for blood. So David acquiesced. They asked that seven sons of Saul be hanged, and David authorized the execution—for the blood that Saul had shed and for the famine that was eating up the land, a famine that God told David resulted from Saul's army taking the lives of the Gibeonites.

And so there on a barren hilltop Rizpah's sons hung, strange fruit from a previous battle. Innocent lives snatched by the state and treated like criminals, their bodies hanging for all to see. But Rizpah, a mother and their defender, took her seat beside the gallows and would not allow the birds of the air or the beasts of the night to consume her sons' flesh. She sat there day after day, waving away the vulture and the coyote, preserving what was left of the sons she loved.

It is the strange consequence of public execution by the state, or with approval or assistance by state authorities, that many are victimized. Black men and women who were lynched were made out to be rapists, abusers, promiscuous, violent, and subjected to a thousand other lying accusations without regard to truth.

Ida B. Wells-Barnett bravely challenged the prevailing justification for lynchings—sexual violations against White women—and declared in her 1909 speech, "Lynching, Our National Crime," that "crimes against women is the excuse, not the cause" of lynching Black people.[1] In her careful documentation of the so-called reasons for lynching, Wells-Barnett uncovered a sweeping variety. Among them are these:

> Keeping saloon, practicing voodooism, political causes, disobeying quarantine regulations, slapping a child, protecting a Negro, knowledge of larceny, writing letter to White woman, asking White woman to marry, jilting girl, having smallpox, concealing criminal, self-defense, insulting language to woman, quarreling with White man, throwing stones, colonizing Negroes . . .[2]

And many other trumped-up charges. And the characterization of the lynched person has all too often imputed predatory and violent sexuality and criminality to them, despite the utter lack of supporting evidence.

Singers Billie Holiday, Nina Simone, and many other mothers have sung of this "Strange Fruit." In 1937, songwriter and poet Abel Meeropol wrote of the poplar trees strewn with the dangling bodies of lynched innocents—blood smeared on leaves and pooling at the base of the trees. Strange fruit, indeed.[3]

Wells-Barnett was no stranger to the personal pain of lynching. When her friend and grocery store owner, Thomas Moss, was lynched along with two of his coworkers, Wells-Barnett used the power of her pen to speak out against lynching. She took on the role of investigative journalist and uncovered the detailed facts about lynchings. She then published her articles under the pen name Iola, to protect her life while she wrote from Memphis for papers all over the nation.[4] Wells-Barnett was undaunted, continuing to reveal the truth in a series of editorials printed in *The New York Age*, led by the well-known African American publisher and writer T. Thomas Fortune.

Ultimately Wells-Barnett printed her findings in *Southern Horrors: Lynch Law in All Its Phases*. This seminal work laid bare the root of accusation that lie at the heart of lynchings: that Black men were "rapists and desperadoes." In a stinging indictment, Wells-Barnett argued in *Southern Horrors* that Black men were at times lynched for having consensual sexual relations with White women, while White men who perpetrated sexual violence against Black women were rarely, if ever, prosecuted.[5] Wells-Barnett's careful research led her to conclude that sexual violence was involved in only about 30 percent of the lynchings of Black men, and that women and children were lynched also.[6]

Wells-Barnett's crusade, like so many other mothers' in the movement for civil rights and for human rights, sought to resurrect the humanity of the murdered and to prevent their lives from being unjustifiably tainted. Like Rizpah, Wells-Barnett fought to protect the memory of the deceased from political and media vultures who would consume the lives of the victims in rumor, innuendo, and bold-faced false accusation.

Devoting an entire chapter in *Southern Horrors* to the lies perpetrated by certain newspapers, Wells-Barnett quotes a writer who accused the Negro race of "having horrible and bestial propensities" that can only be "held in check by speedy and extreme punishment."[7] Wells-Barnett bravely uncovered the violence of lynching to reveal it as the same old racist genocide dressed in the new cry of rape and as a desperate attempt to halt the growing advancement of Black people. In this way she exonerated the vigilantes' victims, the mob-murdered and the street-law sentenced, who were innocent business owners, parents, laborers, house servants, and even the paramours of their accusers. Wells-Barnett proclaimed the widespread slaughter of innocent men, women, and children to be "a blight upon our nation, mocking our laws and disgracing our Christianity."[8]

The most striking parallel to Rizpah's story is Mamie Till Mobley, who courageously, unflinchingly, and sacrificially demanded that the body of her mangled and brutalized son, Emmett Till, be displayed at his funeral. "Let the people see what they did to my boy," Mobley proclaimed despite her acute grief.[9] Surely it was as difficult for her to see her son as it was for Rizpah to watch her own dead sons every day as she chased the birds and wild animals from their decomposing bodies.

Sybrina Fulton, the mother of Trayvon Martin, also raised her hands in faith and her voice in power as she fought to correct the record about the young man who wore a hoodie and carried a bag of skittles when he was shot. Her son was murdered by a so-called neighborhood watcher who was defended in court by the Stand Your Ground law that in some states makes it legal to shoot a person. Trayvon's murderer hunted him down like an animal, though Trayvon was doing nothing but eating candy and walking through the grounds of his dad's Florida apartment complex. Another innocent, he was falsely accused after his murder.

Sybrina Fulton writes in her book *Trayvon: Ten Years Later*,

> It wasn't enough that it took law enforcement far too long to take Trayvon's killer into custody; right-wing conservatives and members of law enforcement started to attack my son's character, as if any mistakes he made as a child could justify his untimely death. I had never seen such a negative frenzy with the media weaponized against the actual victim. We, my family and I, strove to channel our energy in a positive and productive way, but there were times back then when I felt like it was all in vain. It was shameful and undue to see a victim slandered in such a public way.[10]

What could Fulton do in the face of this unjust violence against her son, an injustice rendered legal by a system that had been co-opted by slavery and lynching? First she faced her pain, then she used it as fuel.

> First and foremost, I had my son's name and legacy to protect, and I made it a priority to do so. What was I to do with my anger and hurt? I turned my pain into purpose. I became resolved to change this narrative, to work with victims' families, legislators, communities, and most importantly, our

next young leaders to change minds, heal hearts,
and save lives, and not necessarily in that order.[11]

Fulton spoke up. She spoke out. She started a foundation, the
Trayvon Martin Foundation, to provide emotional and financial
support for families dealing with losses due to gun violence. The
foundation's activities include sharing information about how to
keep people safe as well as how to hold the appropriate people
accountable for the systemic failures at the heart of this all-too-
familiar tragedy. But beyond action and activism, it has been
her faith that has saved her—faith as old as that of Rizpah, who
implored David to give her sons proper burials. As old as Bath-
sheba, who demanded kingship for her son Solomon, and as old
as Mary's mourning for her Son Jesus.

If unjustified vilification is part of public execution, justifiable
shaming is a part of public protest against the unjust. That protest
may be visual and visceral more than it is verbal and rhetorical.
In 1920 thousands of women and men dressed in white paraded
down the streets of New York City in a dramatic silent protest
by the NAACP against Ku Klux Klan violence and American ac-
quiescence to it. In the 1970s women in Chile banged pots and
pans in protest against military dictatorships, a practice known
as the *cacerolazo*, that continues to this day in Europe, Asia, and
North America.

As thousands of protesters took to the streets in the aftermath
of the 2020 suffocation death of George Floyd at the hands of
police, The Wall of Moms in Portland, Oregon, a primarily White
group, linked arms and used their bodies as a shield to stand with
Black Lives Matter demonstrators. That was an act of defiance
against a militarized police force and an act of solidarity with
angered and fed-up Black folk.

Providing resources, compassion, and advocacy to families who
have lost loved ones to violence, Mothers United Against Violence
is a faith-based group of African American women in Hartford,
Connecticut, whose members live out their faith by comforting
the grieving and challenging the guardians of an unjust system.

They and others have all refused to allow injustice to have the last say. Ordinary people demonstrating the power of public outcry and noncooperation with evil always shines a glaring light on those who dishonor, disrespect, and disregard human dignity.

Rizpah's solitary vigil shamed David into doing the right thing.

> When David was told what Aiah's daughter Rispah, Saul's concubine, had done, he went and took the bones of Saul and his son Jonathan from the citizens of Jabesh Gilead. (They had stolen their bodies from the public square at Beth Shan, where the Philistines had hung them after they struck Saul down on Gilboa.) David brought the bones of Saul and his son Jonathan from there, and the bones of those who had been killed and exposed were gathered up.
>
> They buried the bones of Saul and his son Jonathan in the tomb of Saul's father Kish, at Zela in Benjamin, and did everything the king commanded. After that, God answered prayer in behalf of the land. (2 Samuel 21:11–14)

Rizpah's sons were not the only victims of a public execution where the bodies of the dead remained where they had been killed as gruesome reminders of man's bloodthirst. Even King Saul and his son Jonathan could not escape the postwar victory presentation by the Philistines who hung their bodies in public view, only for Saul's and his son's remains to later be stolen by others because no one guards a dead body.

Except, that is, for a mother whose heart still remembers her boys as healthy and vibrant and strong. But there can be no closure, no resolution as long as the wound is open, the strange fruit still hanging. Burial is not so much cover-up as it is a reckoning with the terrible events of execution and a laying to rest of the body, and future descendants. Perhaps it is that a proper burial, complete with its necessary mourning of loss and the acknowledgment of a life, means the planting of a seed of hope that will bring forth new life.

The terrible violence of Saul and his men, not mentioned explicitly by the writer of Samuel or anywhere in the Bible, resulted in famine. There was no rain, no produce. But the burial, the reckoning, restored the broken fellowship with God and healed the land.

Have we reckoned with the violence, the neglect, the unjustified acts of cruelty against Black skin, against Black people?

"If my people, who are called by my name, will humble themselves and pray and seek my face and turn from their wicked ways, then I will hear from heaven, . . . and will heal their land" (2 Chronicles 7:14). The act of burial of Rizpah's relatives was a recognition of human loss, the pain of death, and the sanctity of life. God would then hear the prayers of the people. "After that, God answered prayer in behalf of the land" (2 Samuel 21:14).

Have we reckoned with the violence, the neglect, the unjustified acts of cruelty against Black skin, against Black people? Or do the "bodies" of our victims and our humiliation still hang for public viewing?

Rizpah shamed David into doing the right thing, burying the bones and showing the men the dignity in death that their humanity required. Such burials can be the planting of seeds for the people of faith. Seeds that will not remain buried. What might Ida B. Wells-Barnett say upon discovering that the anti-lynching legislation that she argued for as early as 1898 was finally signed into law by President Joseph Biden on March 29, 2022? How would Mamie Till Mobley, Emmett Till's mother, respond to the enactment of this legislation named for her son? This mother who courageously demanded that the mangled and brutalized body of her son lie in an open casket at his funeral—what would she say? The Emmett Till Antilynching Act introduced by Congressman Bobby Rush finally made lynching a federal crime after nearly two hundred attempts over the years to pass such legislation.[12]

Sybrina Fulton got through the unjust death of her son because of her faith. "I tell [people] to try to hold on to their faith and be strong. Because that is what got me through—my faith."[13] And she continues to fight faithfully for others whose lives were not honored in life or in death, together with the mother of Michael Brown, the mother of Breonna Taylor, the mother of Tamir Rice, the mother of George Floyd. Fulton has stood in faith with the Mothers of the Movement—mothers whose children had been murdered by gun violence: Maria Hamilton, mother of Dontre Hamilton; Lezley McSpadden, mother of Michael Brown; Gwen Carr, mother of Eric Garner; Geneva Reed-Veal, mother of Sandra Bland; Cleopatra Pendleton-Cowley, mother of Hadiya Pendleton; and Lucy McBath, the mother of Jordan Davis.

New life has come forth: new leaders, new voices, new activists—seeds that flower with sweet and powerful fruit. Lucy McBath is now a congresswoman. McBath transitioned from a Delta Airlines flight attendant to national spokesperson for Everytown for Gun Safety and Moms Demand Action for Gun Sense in America after her son was brutally shot and killed by a callous driver who objected to the music Jordan was playing in his car. After seventeen children became victims of gun violence at Parkland High School in Florida, McBath ran for Congress in Georgia's Sixth Congressional District. She won and started drafting gun-safety legislation almost immediately after taking office.[14]

Rizpah, Ida, Sybrina, Lucy, and others know well the power of resurrection for their children and for themselves. Tragedy transformed, depression denied, they refused to let good seed die. Sybrina expresses it this way.

> I didn't pray to become the mother of a movement. I was happy being the mother of Trayvon Martin and Jahvaris Fulton. I became the mother of a movement out of necessity. Sometimes you

have to step into roles you did not ask for and that you do not want. You can find the strength from within if you are willing to live in your purpose. Believe in your strength from within. That's a Word.[15]

Perhaps we, too, are the fruit from the seeds of these women's great faith.

SPEAKING TRUTH TO POWER

Queen Esther / Shaye Moss, Ruby Freeman

And if I perish, I perish.

ESTHER 4:16

Such a time as this . . . such a time
as this . . . it rang in my ears.

A Cloud of Women play

"If I perish," for some, is the possible outcome of speaking truth to power. Not simply idle words, the phrase "If I perish, I perish" was uttered by Queen Esther as she contemplated going to the king of Persia on behalf of her people, the Jews. An evil decree had been written into law allowing all of the Jews to be killed, a decree instituted at the request of one prideful person. His name was Haman. "All the royal officials at the king's gate knelt down and paid honor to Haman, for the king had commanded this concerning him. But Mordecai would not kneel down or pay him honor" (Esther 3:2).

> When Haman saw that Mordecai would not
> kneel down or pay him honor, he was enraged.
> Yet having learned who Mordecai's people were,
> he scorned the idea of killing only Mordecai.

> Instead Haman looked for a way to destroy all
> Mordecai's people, the Jews, throughout the
> whole kingdom of Xerxes. (Esther 3:5–6)

It's hard to understand how someone could transfer his or her feelings for one person to that person's entire ethnic group or religious affiliation. It's hard to believe that human beings are capable of such hatred toward an entire branch of their own human family. Skin color, height, language, customs, faith; all the wonderful aspects of humanity that make the world an exquisite place in which to live for some people become reasons for outrage, subjugation, separation, cruelty, and violence. But Haman's hatred for Mordecai and Mordecai's people is not singular or short-lived. It is a brutal fact of our coexistence on this planet: baseless, ludicrous, and all too real. In Haman's twisted sense of reality, it was not enough to be angry with Mordecai; he ginned up hatred in his own heart, and in the hearts of the Persian people, for every single one of Mordecai's people.

The edict was issued after Haman successfully made his appeal to King Xerxes. All the Jews would be executed throughout Persia. However, Queen Esther, safely behind the palace walls, knew nothing of what was planned for her people. Esther was hiding in plain sight, told by her Uncle Mordecai to keep her identity a secret. Not even the king knew that the woman he had chosen in a national competition to become the new queen was a Jew. Her real name, her Jewish name, was known by no one.

> Dispatches were sent by couriers to all the king's
> provinces with the order to destroy, kill and an-
> nihilate all the Jews—young and old, women
> and children—on a single day, the thirteenth day
> of the twelfth month, the month of Adar, and to
> plunder their goods. (Esther 3:13)

When news of the future slaughter reached Esther's Uncle Mordecai, he took his post outside of the palace walls in sackcloth and ashes and lifted his voice in mourning and weeping together with his fellow Jews throughout the region. Esther sent a messenger outside the gates to dissuade Mordecai from his public outcry only to discover, when the messenger returned, the truth about the planned elimination of the Jews. But Mordecai's response to her concern was not merely an update on the horrible news in the realm. He made a request of Esther that would require her to risk revelation and repudiation—revelation of her true identity, and the repudiation of her crown, or worse, the loss of her life.

> [Mordecai] also gave [Hathak] a copy of the text of the edict for their annihilation, which had been published in Susa, to show to Esther and explain it to her, and he told him to instruct her to go into the king's presence to beg for mercy and plead with him for her people.
>
> Hathak went back and reported to Esther what Mordecai had said. Then she instructed him to say to Mordecai, "All the king's officials and the people of the royal provinces know that for any man or woman who approaches the king in the inner court without being summoned the king has but one law: that they be put to death unless the king extends the gold scepter to them and spares their lives. But thirty days have passed since I was called to go to the king." (Esther 4:8–11)

Mordecai was undeterred. It was time, he told her, time to step out of hiding and speak up.

Mordecai sent this reply to Esther:

> Do not think that because you are in the king's house you alone of all the Jews will escape. For if you remain silent at this time, relief and deliverance for the Jews will arise from another place, but you and your father's family will perish. And

> who knows but that you have come to your royal
> position for such a time as this? (Esther 4:13–14)

Mordecai's question is brilliant. Who knows? Perhaps our particular location in life is part of God's plan. Perhaps the circumstances of our lives serve some greater purpose than our own personal achievement or comfort. Maybe God has been ordering our steps all along, so that we would be where we are, when we need to be there—for the benefit of someone else. Who are you positioned to help?

Who are you positioned to help?

Mordecai's question compelled Esther to think of her position as an undercover Jew in a Persian kingdom in an entirely different way. Who better to go to the king on behalf of the Jews than the queen who is Jewish?

Something happened to Esther in that moment. She encountered that cataclysmic, fear-facing, and fear-overcoming moment when a person realizes that it is time to risk all to speak the truth for the defense and protection of others. In 2022 Shaye Moss and her mother, Ruby Freeman, also experienced that moment.

Seated before the United States House Select Committee on the January 6th attack of 2021, Shaye Moss reported with grace and candor that Republican officials slandered her name, falsely accused her and her mother, and maliciously misrepresented their actions as Georgia state election workers. In the face of death threats these two women spoke truth to power.

Generally speaking, election workers in the twenty-first century probably do not expect to do their work under threat of bodily harm. The events of the previous century paint a different portrait. Black people and their allies in the United States had to fight and march, take to the streets, and argue in court, in order to gain and exercise the right to vote. Women organized and mobilized thousands in order to gain the right to vote. These mass actions that lasted well into the twentieth century were often met by suppression and violence.

We read how Fannie Lou Hamer was nearly beaten to death for organizing people to vote in Mississippi. Congressman John Lewis was nearly beaten to death as he marched from Selma to Montgomery to protest violations and gain voting rights in Alabama. Viola Liuzzo, a volunteer from Detroit, was shot to death by Klansmen as she ferried protestors back to Selma after they reached Montgomery. Jonathan Myrick Daniels, a seminary student from Boston, was murdered by a deputy sheriff after organizing voters in Lowndes County, Mississippi. Finally the passage of voting rights legislation made protecting the right to vote a safer endeavor.

My grandmother, a rather short and determined woman, seemed to grow a couple of inches when it came time to serve as judge of elections for her precinct in Philadelphia, Pennsylvania. I can remember her marching out of her home with some important-looking documents tucked under her arm on her way to her assigned place of service. She and so many other African Americans considered voting an important exercise of civic duty, literally secured by the sacrifice of lives of all colors.

Her increased stature resulted from that sacrifice, her head held high in the legacy of Hamer and Lewis, Liuzzo and Daniels, and countless others. Moss and Freeman, working the elections in the state of Georgia, are also part of that legacy.

Yet after they faithfully served in the 2020 election, their names were attacked, their reputations were maligned, and their lives were threatened based on the manufactured accusations by public officials and those whose candidate lost the presidential election. On January 6, 2021, an estimate of more than two thousand angry protestors stormed the US Capitol at the exact time that the House of Representatives was certifying the tabulated votes in the 2020 election. Backed by unproven claims of election fraud, protestors descended on the Capitol, eventually breaking into the actual building, all while the House and Senate conducted the normally routine certification of electoral votes.[1]

Secret Service personnel quickly evacuated the Senate floor. The protesters broke through the windows. An immediate recess of the Senate was called.

It became the task of the House Select Committee on the January 6th Attack to investigate the fateful events leading up to and taking place on that day. Shaye Moss and her mother found themselves seated in front of a gaggle of photographers and underneath the hot lights as a nation listened to their every word.

"It was just a lot of horrible things there," referring to her Facebook account. "A lot of threats wishing death upon me, telling me I'll be in jail with my mother and saying things like, 'Be glad it's 2020 and not 1920.'" Ms. Moss and Ms. Freeman were publicly accused of fraudulent counting practices and illegal activity. Ruby Freeman said: "I won't even introduce myself by my name anymore. I get nervous when I bump into someone I know in the grocery store who says my name. I'm worried about people listening. I get nervous when I have to give my name for food orders. I'm always concerned of who's around me."[2]

Shaye Moss shared, "This turned my life upside down. I no longer give out my business card. I don't transfer calls. I—I don't want anyone knowing my name. I don't want to go anywhere with my mom because she might yell my name out over the grocery aisle or something. I don't go to the grocery store at all. I haven't been anywhere at all."

Our names speak family history and present reality. Name-robbing is one of the ways to destroy, demean, and diminish a people's culture. Africans brought to this country as slaves were given names that spoke of subservience and dehumanization and were robbed of names that connected them to African culture and history. One of the first things many emancipated slaves did was to take a new name.[3] It was an act of self-determination and many times the selection of a new name was intended as a deliberate separation from one's slave identity. The threat of violence forced Shaye Moss and her mother to hide their names, to surrender their identity to preserve their lives, to disconnect from family and community.

Oppressed people have often been forced into the shape-shifting practice of identity alteration. Hiding in plain sight has been a liberation strategy and survival mechanism. Frederick

Douglass escaped from slavery by pretending to be the person whose papers he presented to authorities. Many modern-day Jewish descendants of Queen Esther altered their names and often hid their religion upon escape from the Holocaust. Belle da Costa Greene, the famed personal librarian of J.P. Morgan, added da Costa and Cuban heritage to her name, to explain her tan skin so that she could travel the world purchasing rare books as the White female representative of New York's prestigious Morgan Library.[4]

Sojourner Truth, however, in an act of defiance and definition, took the name of Sojourner Truth as part of her God-ordained calling in life; "Sojourner because I was to travel up and down the land showing people their sins and being a sign to them, and Truth because I was to declare the Truth unto the people."[5] Names are a sacred truth, and Shaye Moss and Ruby Freeman were violently forced to capitulate theirs; but like Queen Esther, only for a season.

The fact that they testified at all is its own story. These African American women gave sworn testimony before a House Committee at the center of, arguably, one of the most controversial chapters in recent American history. They found the courage and strength to speak the truth about who they are and the tragic circumstances they encountered. Like Queen Esther generations earlier, they met the fear-overcoming moment with the courage of their convictions. Shaye Moss and Ruby Freeman exposed a crime against the innocent, and so did Queen Esther. She found the strength to reveal her Jewish identity to the king for the deliverance of her people.

> Then Esther sent this reply to Mordecai: "Go, gather together all the Jews who are in Susa, and fast for me. Do not eat or drink for three days, night or day. I and my attendants will fast as you do. When this is done, I will go to the king, even though it is against the law. And if I perish, I perish." (Esther 4:15–16)

Suddenly Esther became a commander. Summoning the strength to risk personal privilege for salvation and deliverance of the innocent, she called on the wailing community to fast on her behalf. She accepted her role as advocate but understood her need for spiritual power to go before the king. Long before the physical encounter with King Xerxes of Persia, the Jewish people had experienced a faith encounter with the King of kings, the God who saw them in bondage in Egypt and heard their cries.

> I have indeed seen the misery of my people in Egypt. I have heard them crying out because of their slave drivers, and I am concerned about their suffering. So I have come down to rescue them from the hand of the Egyptians and to bring them up out of that land into a good and spacious land, a land flowing with milk and honey—the home of the Canaanites, Hittites, Amorites, Perizzites, Hivites and Jebusites. And now the cry of the Israelites has reached me, and I have seen the way the Egyptians are oppressing them. So now, go. I am sending you to Pharaoh to bring my people the Israelites out of Egypt. (Exodus 3:7–10)

Cries of lament were turned to cries for God's strength, and for God to use the orphan turned Queen to throw down her crown and go to the king. But the Queen learned well the lesson of preparation. For a year, she had prepared with oils and baths to go before the king in the hope of becoming the queen. She prepared once again, while the Jews' lives hung in the balance, to go before him in contravention of the law. Armed with courage and faith in an unseen God, she put on the attire of her station and waited for an audience with the king. In this book of the Bible God's voice does not boom from heaven; there is not a cloud of smoke to lead by day or a cloud of fire to lead by night. God's name is not even mentioned. Yet the real living

God does arise in this story. The God of deliverance is, in fact, neither absent nor uncaring.

After Queen Esther stood before the king, in that perilous moment when her life hung in the balance, he extended the royal scepter and welcomed her to come near to his throne. This picture of a hidden exile, a dressed-up foreigner, an orphan, being welcomed into the throne room of the king is great symbolism for those who must speak truth to power. There is a welcome for the people of God to come to the Lord with the cries of injustice.

Esther was not the only one vindicated in the book called after her name. Uncle Mordecai was honored by the king for saving the king's life from traitors in the kingdom. When Esther revealed her identity to the king, she also revealed Haman as the architect of the attack against the Jews, and the king himself ordered Haman's execution. Haman was hanged on the gallows he had built to hang Mordecai.

> Then Queen Esther answered, "If I have found favor with you, Your Majesty, and if it pleases you, grant me my life—this is my petition. And spare my people—this is my request. For I and my people have been sold to be destroyed, killed and annihilated. If we had merely been sold as male and female slaves, I would have kept quiet, because no such distress would justify disturbing the king."
>
> King Xerxes asked Queen Esther, "Who is he? Where is he—the man who has dared to do such a thing?"
>
> Esther said, "An adversary and enemy! This vile Haman!"
>
> Then Haman was terrified before the king and queen. (Esther 7:3–6)

Though Haman literally begged the queen for his life, the king was not persuaded by his words this time. The one who urged the king to condemn the Jews faced condemnation himself. Then the king reversed the edict to annihilate the Jews.

> On the thirteenth day of the twelfth month, the month of Adar, the edict commanded by the king was to be carried out. On this day the enemies of the Jews had hoped to overpower them, but now the tables were turned and the Jews got the upper hand over those who hated them. (Esther 9:1)

It turns out that the heart of the king could be moved. It turns out that the king did take action to protect the lives and future of the Jewish people. It turns out that the king still cared about his queen though she was a Jew from a broken family.

It turns out that courage demands truth. Can we challenge the lie without revealing the truth of who we really are? Can injustice be fought without standing in the light? Shaye Moss and Ruby Freeman were terrorized into hiding their names, but because of their courage now everyone knows their names.

In the biblical record, God calls people by their names: Abraham, Hagar, Moses, Jacob, Samuel, Paul, Mary, Martha, Simon, and more. The great God and creator of the universe knows us by name. We are not simply numbers or moments in time, but people with purpose and destiny that come directly from the throne room in heaven. Hagar was told her son would have many descendants. Moses was told to lead the people to freedom. Paul was told to stop persecuting the followers of Jesus. Abram was told he would be the father of nations. His name, God said, would be great because he was to be the first of many.

> The LORD had said to Abram, "Go from your country, your people and your father's household to the land I will show you.
>
> "I will make you into a great nation,
>   and I will bless you;

> I will make your name great,
>> and you will be a blessing.
> I will bless those who bless you,
>> and whoever curses you I will curse;
> and all peoples on earth
>> will be blessed through you." (Genesis 12:1–3)

Will there not also be greatness in the lives of Abram's children? Will not the descendants also be blessed?

Ruby Freeman said, "I've always believed it when God says that he'll make your name great, but this is not the way it was supposed to be. I could have never imagined the events that followed the presidential election 2020."

But God did make her name great, and that of her daughter. Believing in God, two women came out of hiding and publicly challenged a violent and nefarious group of people, disclosing information that shocked the nation, and powerfully informed the public about previously unknown events. In the tradition of Esther, one of only two women after whom a book of the Bible is named, God makes great the names of those with the courage to reveal their names in the fight for truth.

WE WANT PEACE!

Abigail / The Peace Women of Liberia

Please forgive your servant's presumption. The LORD your God will certainly make a lasting dynasty for my lord, because you fight the LORD's battles, and no wrongdoing will be found in you as long as you live. Even though someone is pursuing you to take your life, the life of my lord will be bound securely in the bundle of the living by the LORD your God, but the lives of your enemies he will hurl away as from the pocket of a sling. When the LORD has fulfilled for my lord every good thing he promised concerning him and has appointed him ruler over Israel, my lord will not have on his conscience the staggering burden of needless bloodshed or of having avenged himself. And when the LORD your God has brought my lord success, remember your servant.

1 SAMUEL 25:28–31

I was married to an evil man, a man I was afraid
to fight. Despite his arrogant ways, David came
to help him and our entire clan. Yet even with
David, he was belligerent and selfish. I had to save
him, and myself; David, I knew, was a warrior
and would not take kindly to his insults. So I
intervened, in the only way I knew how . . .

A Cloud of Women play

It is not war that stops war. It is peace. In the country of Liberia the fourteen-year war was stopped by the power of God and the women of peace. And they started with prayer.

To Leymah Gbowee, it seemed that the fighting had been going on forever. As the rebel forces moved closer to Monrovia, a certain kind of fervent righteous indignation began to take hold of groups of women. As far back as 1994 the Liberian Women's Initiative called for protests and strikes in opposition to war.

Gather the women to pray for peace!

The Mano River Union Women's Peace Network was engaging in the push for peace in the region. Peace work was taking place among the women. They felt a calling to address the war because clearly the men were either unable or unwilling to do so. But God seemed to be issuing a more urgent call.

> And that spring, in the office, I had a dream. I didn't know where I was. Everything was dark. I couldn't see a face, but I heard a voice, and it was talking to me—commanding me: "Gather the women to pray for peace!" Gather the women to pray for peace! I could still hear echoes as I woke up, shaking. It was 5 A.M.[1]

Leymah Gbowee had recently begun working for the Women in Peace Building Network (WIPNET), a newer women's peace organization. She did not expect God to speak *to* her or *through* her. She was, like so many of us, struggling to live a Christian life. Yet when others around her heard the words from her dream they agreed: God was calling the women to pray—together. That moment became a new starting point and that dream became the Christian Women's Peace Initiative.

In June 2002 a weekly women's noontime prayer meeting began, and as word of the effort spread, others gathered to pray as well. It soon became clear to those praying and those organizing in WIPNET that it was time to act. Training was first on the agenda: advocacy, mediation, and political organizing were combined with relationship-building. Personal truths were shared confidentially in an exercise called "Shedding the Weight." Victories and challenges were shared during "Crown and Thorns." Women from different backgrounds joined together as a fierce team fighting for peace. In perhaps the most shocking development, Muslim women leaders joined the Christian women leaders to bring both groups of women together to push for peace. A new slogan emerged, "Does the bullet know Christian from Muslim? Does the bullet pick and choose?"[2]

A December 2002 march demonstrated the united purpose of the women of Liberia. Two hundred Christian and Muslim women marched the streets in the capital city of Monrovia declaring with their presence and the statement they issued: "We envision Peace." That vision was increasingly threatened by the rebel forces that continued to move violently and ruthlessly toward the capital. Finally in April of 2003 a barbaric attack just outside Monrovia catapulted the women to force the hand of President Taylor, whose cruel regime and heartless military tactics had terrorized the country. One thousand women stood on the steps of the capitol stating they had a document to present to President Taylor. He did not appear but the media did and gave the women's movement purposeful visibility and gravitas.

So the women sat down. Selecting a field that Taylor's motorcade passed twice each day, more than two thousand women dressed in white as a sign of peace and sat there for the entire day. In the hot baking sun and in the drenching rain, they sat. That first day and every day for weeks and weeks from dusk to dawn, their placards declaring one clear message, "We want peace—no more war!" When Taylor finally did respond to one of several three-day ultimatums given by the women, he agreed to participate in peace talks, but he challenged the women to encourage the rebels to participate as well, a challenge the women met with determination and faith.

The women of Liberia harnessed a power that was undeniable, even by the men who daily disrespected them. These mothers, aunties, and grandmothers looked not only to that current moment of war and devastation, but to the war's impact on future generations. They stood up and spoke out and sat down to rescue the future from the hell of today. Abigail, a woman whose story is told in the Old Testament, also had her eye on the future when she averted a war between King David and his soldiers, and her husband Nabal and his shepherds.

David and his men, living in the wilderness, were on the run from Saul who repeatedly tried to take David's life. When David heard that Nabal's shepherds were nearby shearing sheep, David sent ten young men to request food from Nabal to supply David's band of warriors. Nabal was a wealthy landowner who could easily afford to share his bounty, but Nabal was cruel and stingy and refused David's men.

> Nabal answered David's servants, "Who is this David? Who is this son of Jesse? Many servants are breaking away from their masters these days. Why should I take my bread and water, and the meat I have slaughtered for my shearers, and give it to men coming from who knows where?" (1 Samuel 25:10–11)

David was incensed when he heard Nabal's words. He commanded his men to take up their swords, and four hundred men descended on Nabal's property. Abigail, Nabal's wife, had gotten wind of the plan from one of the shepherds and she acted immediately. She had loaves and wine, sheep and figs loaded onto donkeys and sent by messenger to David and his men. When she arrived she got on her knees before David and began to appeal to his future, the future that God had ordained for him, a future that would surely have been darkened and destroyed by the blood he vowed to shed.

> When Abigail saw David, she quickly got off her donkey and bowed down before David with her face to the ground. She fell at his feet and said:

> "Pardon your servant, my lord, and let me speak
> to you; hear what your servant has to say. . . .
> "Please forgive your servant's presumption.
> The LORD your God will certainly make a last-
> ing dynasty for my lord, because you fight the
> LORD's battles, and no wrongdoing will be
> found in you as long as you live." (1 Samuel
> 25:23–24, 28)

Abigail spoke not to David's current reality or the conflict of the present moment; Abigail spoke to David's dynasty, the generations that were yet to come.

> Even though someone is pursuing you to take
> your life, the life of my lord will be bound se-
> curely in the bundle of the living by the LORD
> your God, but the lives of your enemies he will
> hurl away as from the pocket of a sling. (v. 29)

Abigail declared God's protection over David, and that the Lord would deal with the enemies of David.

> When the LORD has fulfilled for my lord every
> good thing he promised concerning him and has
> appointed him ruler over Israel, my lord will not
> have on his conscience the staggering burden of
> needless bloodshed or of having avenged himself.
> And when the LORD your God has brought my
> lord success, remember your servant. (vv. 30–31)

Abigail addressed David as the future ruler of Israel. She spoke of the possible ramifications of the acts of violence he was contemplating, and the conflict of a bloody conscience with godly leadership. Her words did not derive simply from her own logic and good sense. In that brief time period, Abigail had become the voice of God articulating God's purposes for David—and for

Israel. It was this call to yield personal purpose, benefit, and gain to God's purpose for the people and the nation that moved David's heart and awakened him to a different outcome, an alternative to simple ruthless revenge.

> David said to Abigail, "Praise be to the LORD, the God of Israel, who has sent you today to meet me. May you be blessed for your good judgment and for keeping me from bloodshed this day and from avenging myself with my own hands. Otherwise, as surely as the LORD, the God of Israel, lives, who has kept me from harming you, if you had not come quickly to meet me, not one male belonging to Nabal would have been left alive by daybreak."
>
> Then David accepted from her hand what she had brought him and said, "Go home in peace. I have heard your words and granted your request." (vv. 32–35)

Had Abigail not moved when she did, had Abigail waited for some other hero or some other rescue, David may have gone forward with his murderous plot. Her words and generosity melted the stony heart of offense just in the nick of time. The peace women of Liberia made a similar impact on Charles Taylor and on the rebel fighters.

Peace talks between the Liberians United for Reconciliation and Democracy (LURD) fighters and President Taylor would not take place until a mutually satisfactory location could be arranged. Without meaningful peace talks soon, the women knew that the war would escalate. Three key women from Women of Liberia Mass Action for Peace arranged to join the meetings between LURD representatives and the Liberian Council of Churches. They characterized themselves as the mothers and sisters of the men. They spoke of the long journey they'd taken to speak with them and, like Abigail, they spoke to their future potential rather than their current reality.

"You're such important men," an experienced organizer named Sugars declared. "Everyone depends on you to save Liberia."[3] She did not speak of any personal benefit that the LURD representatives would gain from attending the peace talks or ending the war; her message was about the role these men could play in saving the nation from a ravaged and desolate future.

Persuaded by the women, the LURD fighters did decide to go to Ghana for the peace talks, but there was yet more work for the peace women to do. The women met in the hundreds at the site of the peace talks, at times standing outside in the rain and refusing to be moved to a covered location. As the peace talks dragged on the women grew weary of warlords sleeping in comfortable hotel rooms and eating and drinking as though on vacation while the suffering of the citizens increased with new acts of barbarity taking place daily.

With no discernible agreement in sight the women took direct action; they locked arms and took their stance surrounding the meeting location, declaring that they would hold the men captive inside the hall until an agreement was reached. When the security officials threatened to have them removed, Leymah Gbowee began disrobing, which is traditionally believed to cause a curse to fall on any man who sees a married or elderly woman bare herself. Tensions flared and the women began to cry out because of the suffering in Liberia.

Eventually a statement was read to the press allowing the peace talks to proceed but making clear that the women would continue their presence in protest outside of the talks and would take extreme action again if the need arose. About three weeks later, Charles Taylor resigned and the Accra Comprehensive Peace Agreement was signed August 18, 2003, creating a new transitional government.

Back in Liberia the peace women were met at the airport with shouting, "These were the peace women! These were the women who did great work. Thank you, mothers. Thank you."[4]

Will the world heed the voices of the peace women? Can we afford not to? We want peace—no more war!

COME INTO MY HOUSE AND STAY

Lydia / Bridget "Biddy" Mason, Lisette Denison Forth

> After Paul and Silas came out of the prison, they
> went to Lydia's house, where they met with the
> brothers and sisters and encouraged them.
> ACTS 16:40

> I know how to run my house.
> *A Cloud of Women* play

On my first mission trip to Africa, I (Georgia) stayed at the home of two sisters in a village in Tanzania. They were chicken farmers and they welcomed me and another young woman as their overnight guests. We slept in a room off the kitchen and were awakened, of course, by the rooster's early morning call. Breakfast was thick wheat bread and very, very fresh eggs. Just as we were about to eat our bread, one of the sisters stood on a chair and reached into the very back of a cabinet. She pulled out a small jar of honey she had clearly been saving for a special occasion and set it before us on the table. We might as well have spread gold dust on our bread, so precious and delicious was this one small jar of honey. It was generosity and love that they served that day. I will always remember that visit and their kindness. We experienced great hospitality because they opened their house to us—*their house.*

A father's house. The "house of the father"—*beit av*—is a powerful term in the Old Testament. It suggests much more than a physical location. The term actually refers to the people who live in the house. In the ancient Near East families lived together, with tents or rooms that connected. Living was communal, multigenerational, and identified by the father as the head of the clan. Sometimes the phrase *house of the father* was used to describe a particular tribe or the generations that would ultimately come from that patriarch. References to the house of David, that greatly revered king of Israel, are classic examples of this broader meaning of "house of the father."

> Nevertheless, because of the covenant the LORD
> had made with David, the LORD was not willing
> to destroy the house of David. He had promised
> to maintain a lamp for him and his descendants
> forever. (2 Chronicles 21:7)

Yes, the father has a house but what about the mother? What about the countless mothers who have cooked, washed, cleaned, filled, fixed, held up, covered up, paid up, prayed over, and cried over houses holding kids and grandkids, cousins and kin from near and from far? *Don't they also have houses?*

How shall we name the lineage of mothers and grandmothers who raise generations without fathers, including perhaps even Mary the mother of Jesus?

The irony is that for many ancient and modern cultures the house has been the province of women—to clean and maintain, to fill and feed, and follow the patter of little feet. The adage told little girls growing up has been, "Women's work is never done." So although women worked tirelessly in the house, particularly during the period of time when the events of the Bible took place, the "house" was named for the father. Apparently sweat equity contributes little value in the calculus of lineage naming.

The Bible does record the "houses" of some women. God

gives houses to Shiphrah and Puah, those Hebrew midwives who refused to murder the boys as Pharaoh had commanded them.

> The king of Egypt said to the Hebrew midwives, whose names were Shiphrah and Puah, "When you are helping the Hebrew women during child-birth on the delivery stool, if you see that the baby is a boy, kill him; but if it is a girl, let her live." The midwives, however, feared God and did not do what the king of Egypt had told them to do; they let the boys live. Then the king of Egypt summoned the midwives and asked them, "Why have you done this? Why have you let the boys live?"
>
> The midwives answered Pharaoh, "Hebrew women are not like Egyptian women; they are vig-orous and give birth before the midwives arrive."
>
> So God was kind to the midwives and the people increased and became even more numer-ous. And because the midwives feared God, he gave them families of their own. (Exodus 1:15–21)

It is interesting to note that in verse twenty-one, the Hebrew word *beit* (house) is translated "families" in a number of Bible versions: New International Version, New Living Translation, English Standard Version, New Revised Standard Version, Christian Standard Bible, and others. In other words, the powerful meaning of *house* which includes related families, clan, tribe, and lineage is not captured in this word as it applies to women. This story of the Hebrew midwives connects their righteous acts to having *families* but in truth their progeny includes *generations*, the descendants of boys whose lives they saved. The houses of these women continue to stretch into the future, houses built by faith and defiance and courage.

And the color purple.

> And on the Sabbath day we went outside the gate to a riverside, where we were thinking that there was a place of prayer; and we sat down and began speaking to the women who had assembled.
>
> A woman named Lydia was listening; she was a seller of purple fabrics from the city of Thyatira, and a worshiper of God. The Lord opened her heart to respond to the things spoken by Paul. Now when she and her household had been baptized, she urged us, saying, "If you have judged me to be faithful to the Lord, come into my house and stay." And she prevailed upon us.
> (Acts 16:13–15 NASB)

Lydia is that rare example of an independent businesswoman in the Bible. The purple fabric she sold was valuable because it was created with a costly dye that came from a particular shellfish. It could take up to ten thousand shellfish to create just a small amount of this dye.[1] Quite often worn by rulers and the wealthy, purple fabric commanded a hefty price so Lydia was a person of means.

Lydia is also a leader in her household, a household that likely included staff or servants in addition to children. There is no mention of a husband or a father. Some scholars believe that Lydia may have been a freed woman. Some of the sellers of purple were freed slaves who supported their families through this trade. Whatever the reason, Lydia is not associated with a male figure; the fact that only women were gathered at the riverside may be evidence that there were not enough men to form a synagogue. Without ten men to initiate a synagogue, Jewish believers would form small gatherings near fresh water so that the rituals of purification could still take place.[2]

Lydia was a businesswoman but on that day her main business was faith. She came to the riverside because she believed in God and the God she sought opened her heart to hear. Without male teachers there at the riverside Paul's teaching would likely have been a welcome addition to the time of gathering. But Paul was not teaching Mosaic law that day. He spoke of the One called Jesus and Lydia believed. There at the river's edge, the waters of ritual became the waters of liberation and Lydia gathered her entire household to join the Way of Christ. And immediately she opened her house to the men who shared Good News.

Hospitality for many communities in the world is an absolute necessity, even today. The offer of house and home made it possible to travel places that might otherwise be completely forbidding. The Gospel of Jesus Christ spread first from house to house and village to village. Places to rest and refresh were invaluable for the apostles and those who traveled with them carrying the teachings of Jesus. In the American South a people freed from slavery but still plagued by racial violence developed networks of safe houses, places to lodge for travelers going north or west. In communities where lodging is rare or dangerous, hospitality continues to provide the shelter needed to continue one's journey.

As a baptized believer Lydia was determined to serve. Hospitality was highly valued in the ancient Near East, so her decision to open her home would not have been unusual except that she welcomed those who were in conflict with Roman law and were the victims of persecution. Opening her home to the followers of Jesus Christ exposed her to risk, but she wasted no time in extending the offer to Paul and Silas.

She invited them to abide, to stay, from the Greek word *meno*. This term has significant meaning as can be seen in John's gospel when Jesus encourages believers to *abide* in Him and He will *abide* in them (John 15:4). Jesus invites believers to find their rest in Him and to remain connected. As such Jesus is admonishing them to maintain the connection to Him, as a branch remains connected to the life-giving vine. Without this connection, Jesus warns, there will be no fruitfulness. So when Lydia invites Paul and Silas to abide with her, she is inviting them to more than just a place to sleep and grab a meal; she is offering them a place of Christian rest and gathering. This gesture invites them to the earliest form of ecclesiastical gathering: house church.

Lydia's house was resting place and shelter, as well as gathering place and strategic nerve center for the continuation of the gospel mission. Her simple gesture of hospitality literally opened the door for the word of Jesus Christ to spread to the European continent—and it started from a humble gathering of women on the banks of a river. The unpredictable and surprising outcome, and far-reaching impact, of a gathered few and the small investment of a woman of faith. "Do not despise these small beginnings, for the LORD rejoices to see the work begin" (Zechariah 4:10 NLT).

> **When Lydia invites Paul and Silas to abide with her, . . . she is offering them a place of Christian rest and gathering.**

It was a long walk. Born into slavery in 1818, Bridget "Biddy" Mason was the workhorse of Robert and Rebecca Smith, who forced her to walk from Mississippi to Utah behind their wagon caravan herding sheep and other animals. After several years her slaveholders moved to California and Biddy Mason was forced to walk again. When she and her three children arrived in California, she tried to run away from her owners but was caught and returned to the couple who continued to enslave her against her will and against the law. California was a free state but Biddy Mason was denied her freedom. She may have been bound by physical slavery, but Biddy Mason was not bound in her soul. She spoke of being free so when her owners decided to return to the South, Biddy's free Black acquaintances contacted the sheriff who arrested her and placed her in *protective* custody![3]

In an unprecedented series of events, Biddy was presented before the judge under a writ of habeas corpus, compelling the Smiths to articulate their reasons for keeping her a slave. They claimed they were not holding her as a slave but that she was joining them of her own free will. When her attorney failed to appear in court, Judge Benjamin Hayes heard Biddy Mason's testimony in chambers, deftly avoiding the potential legal conflict of having a "slave" give testimony in open court. It was illegal for a slave to testify. Biddy Mason said what she already knew to be true: that she was free and did not want to go South with the Smiths. Judge Hayes's ruling in her favor sounded almost biblical.

> And it further appearing by satisfactory proof to the judge here, that all of the said persons of color are entitled to their freedom, and are free and cannot be held in slavery or involuntary servitude, it is therefore argued that they are entitled to their freedom and are free forever (State of California, County of Los Angeles, Before the Hon. Benjamin Hayes, Judge of the District Court of the First Judicial District State of California, County of Los Angeles, January 19, 1856).

Bridget Biddy Mason, freewoman, gained and spread wealth. She delivered babies, supported families, provided for neighbors in distress, and purchased a home in what is now downtown Los Angeles. She overcame barriers, stigma, bondage, and bias, eventually amassing wealth that would make her a multimillionaire by today's standards.

According to the ACLU of Northern California,

> Bridget Mason became a doctor's assistant and ran a midwifing business. She accumulated a fortune worth about $7.5 million in today's dollars, making her one of the richest women in Los Angeles. She established a homestead in what became downtown Los Angeles. Mason used her wealth to establish a daycare center for working parents and created an account at a store where families who lost their homes in flooding could get supplies.[4]

Like Lydia, Bridget Mason opened a house, and this house became known as First African Methodist Episcopal Church (FAME).

Biddy Mason took the wealth that she gained and funded a church. She took the faith that she had and made her vision a reality. This former slave bought land and used her freedom to extend help and hope to others. Today FAME opens its doors to more than nineteen thousand members. With finances she earned from her various enterprises, Biddy Mason bought land and provided funding for the church. She was a landowner at a time when African American women were struggling to exercise the few, if any, rights they had. She even funded what came to be known as the first parking lot in Los Angeles.

From inauspicious beginnings as a slave who walked nearly two thousand miles, she refused to allow her condition of servitude to limit her future reality of freedom. She spoke up for herself and gave herself in service to others. Her faith carried her to places that seemed impossible but her open arms and open heart invited others to come to her house and stay.

There is a park in downtown Los Angeles named for her: Biddy Mason Memorial Park. And in that park there is a wall, a concrete wall that tells the story of her life. Artist Sheila Levrant de Bretteville created "Biddy Mason: Time and Place," designed with stamped impressions of objects that signify moments in Biddy's life. This concrete testimony to the events of a life of faith and freedom reminds us that mothers do have houses, and generations that remember open doors.

It was an unlikely friendship. Elizzbeth "Lisette" Denison's life is also remembered in brick and mortar in the small island community of Grosse Ile, Michigan. The island lies just south of the city of Detroit, wedged between the city's southern suburbs and the coast of Canada. Home today to just over ten thousand residents, Grosse Ile has never been home to large numbers of African Americans. Growing up in the city of Detroit, we never had a reason to go there. I don't remember hearing any Black folks talk about having friends or family on Grosse Ile. I have only been there twice. Although there is lots of water in the Detroit area, the bridge to Grosse Ile just pops up unexpectedly on the road and takes one to a lovely island with views of Canada and also of

118

industry that thoughtlessly pours its waste into the waters in that part of metro Detroit.

On my second visit to Grosse Ile, I toured St. James Episcopal Church as part of a clergy gathering and was surprised to discover that this predominantly White church in a predominantly White city had been started through the unlikely friendship between Lisette Denison Forth, an African American and former slave, and Eliza Biddle, a White woman married to a prominent elected official in the region.

Lisette Denison was born into slavery in Macomb County, Michigan, named after the slaveholding Macomb family. When the will of her parents' owner, a British loyalist, declared the parents to be free but Lisette and her siblings to remain slaves, Mr. and Mrs. Denison took the brave and unusual step to sue for the freedom of their six children. Complex legalities regarding the ownership of slaves by British citizens and other technicalities became the legal foundation that Judge Woodward relied upon to rule that Lisette and two of her brothers would be slaves forever, and that one brother would be free after twenty-five years of enslavement.[5]

The Denisons would not give up. They continued to fight for the freedom of their children, following the path that countless slaves before them had taken, traveling from midnight to dawn on what was known as the Underground Railroad. Detroit, on the shores of the gateway to freedom, was known as "Midnight" and a settlement near the city of Windsor, Canada, came to be known as "Dawn."

> Before the Civil War, more than 30,000 people crossed into Canada, many of them from Midnight to Dawn, some more than once as they returned to help others. . . . It is a story of desperation and resistance, of courage and survival, of men and women who risked their lives in order to claim the life that they, and they alone, owned.[6]

Leaving behind employment and the faint glimmer of financial independence in Michigan, the Denisons packed up their family and departed for the country of Canada where they could all finally be free. With a changed status and renewed hope, they later returned to the Detroit area to live their lives as free people.

During her lifetime Lisette amassed funds in ways that are surprising for a former slave. She purchased land in Pontiac, Michigan, making her the first African American and one of the first women to own property in the state. She made financial gains by investing her earnings in stocks and in a cruising steamboat company. If her business dealings made her a rare occurrence, her friendship with Eliza Biddle may have been rarer still.

In 1831 Lisette joined the household of John Biddle, mayor of Detroit and founder of Wyandotte, Michigan, working as a domestic houseworker. During this time, Lisette purchased a home in Detroit and started reaping profits from her business ventures. Lisette traveled to Paris with the Biddle family at the request of Biddle's wife, Eliza. The two women developed a friendship revealed later in letters written by Eliza Biddle to others. It's not likely that she would have written to Lisette because Lisette could neither read nor write yet the two women from very different backgrounds shared a common faith. Lisette had a dream to start a church for both rich and poor and she shared her dream with her friend Eliza. The two women, both Episcopalians, made a vow to eventually build a chapel.

The two Biddle sons worked together to bring Lisette's dream to reality, the dream of a slave freed by escaping to Canada. After the death of their mother, one brother contributed additional funding and the other brother donated the land. Two years after Lisette Denison Forth passed away, the first church service was held at St. James Episcopal Church.[7] Her vision for a church was fulfilled, a place where believers from different backgrounds could gather, find rest, and abide. Perhaps her own friendship with Eliza Biddle was exemplary of the words of the apostle Paul to the Galatian church. "There is neither Jew nor Gentile, neither slave nor free, nor is there male and female, for you are all one in Christ Jesus"

(Galatians 3:28). Lisette Denison Forth envisioned a church where all would be welcome no matter the status or stature.

> Having long felt the inadequacy of the provisions made for the poor in our houses of worship, and knowing from sad experience that many devout believers and humble followers of the lowly Jesus are excluded from those courts, where the rich and poor should meet together, shut out from those holy services by the mammon of unrighteousness, from that very church which declares the widow's mite to be more acceptable in the sight of the Lord than the careless offerings of those who give of their "abundance." . . . I therefore now give and bequeath to William S. Biddle of the City of Detroit all the rest of my estate of whatever nature it may be . . . to be used in the erection of a fine chapel for the use of the Protestant Episcopal Church of which I am a communicant.[8]

Visitors to St. James enter the church through bright red doors that are dedicated to the church's founder. A nearby plaque reads,

> THESE DOORS ARE GIVEN
> TO THE GLORY OF GOD
> IN LOVING MEMORY OF
> ELIZABETH DENISON FORTH
> WHO WILLED HER LIFE SAVINGS
> THAT THIS CHURCH MIGHT BE BUILT

Lisette never saw the church of her dreams. She never sat in its pews or talked to its people, but the invitation she extended still calls to those who seek the One, and the doors she envisioned still open to those who wish to enter.

A house that welcomes the faithless and the faithful, the lost, the lonely, the content, and the critic, is also women's work.

From Lydia's simple gesture of hospitality came the beginnings of European Christianity, and from a kind welcome to itinerant evangelists came the earliest gathering of what later came to be known as the church at Philippi.

Lydia's invitation to Paul and Silas was accepted. Her vision, like that of Bridget Biddy Mason and Lisette Denison Forth, of having believers gather in the house became a reality when Paul and Silas visited Lydia's home after they had been released from jail.

> But Paul said to the officers: "They beat us publicly without a trial, even though we are Roman citizens, and threw us into prison. And now do they want to get rid of us quietly? No! Let them come themselves and escort us out."
>
> The officers reported this to the magistrates, and when they heard that Paul and Silas were Roman citizens, they were alarmed. They came to appease them and escorted them from the prison, requesting them to leave the city. After Paul and Silas came out of the prison, they went to Lydia's house, where they met with the brothers and sisters and encouraged them. Then they left. (Acts 16:37–40)

No longer a simple visit by two followers of Jesus Christ to her home, the time of gathering now included other believers who had come to meet Paul and Silas. The place of rest and abiding became a place of encouraging and sharing the Good News of Jesus Christ: a house of hope and open doors, then and still.

NAMED AND NAMELESS WOMEN WHO LOVED JESUS

Mary Magdalene / Many Others

> After this, Jesus traveled about from one town and village to another, proclaiming the good news of the kingdom of God. The Twelve were with him, and also some women who had been cured of evil spirits and diseases: Mary (called Magdalene) from whom seven demons had come out; Joanna the wife of Chuza, the manager of Herod's household; Susanna; and many others. These women were helping to support them out of their own means.
>
> LUKE 8:1–3

> Women of spirit, women of witness
> come out from the shadows
> show us your heart.
>
> *A Cloud of Women* play

In truth, there were women disciples. Followers of Jesus who opened their homes, prepared the meals, sewed the clothes, bought the food, sold their wares, and contributed money. Yet the female followers of Jesus throughout history have fallen to the same reductionism as women everywhere. Hips rather than history have become their hallmark. So it is with Mary Magdalene, who has been characterized as a woman of dubious character, promiscuous, a harlot, despite the fact that her past is described only as "delivered of 7 demons."[1]

The cable series *The Chosen*, a dramatization of the life and community of Jesus Christ, illustrated this moment of deliverance so well. A woman tormented by darkness deep within encounters a man who calls her by her birth name. As she cries, Jesus reaches for her. The embrace, the loving acceptance of the Messiah, transforms a shattered "Lilith" (her street name) into a liberated Mary of Magdala, free to serve and follow Him.

Mary Magdalene is a genuine eyewitness to the transformative power of Jesus Christ. His ministry was not a tale she had heard, it was an experience she had lived. She followed Jesus Christ because she knew what redeeming love could do. Yet she was often referred to as a woman of the evening, a regenerated harlot. This description arose out of the practice of connecting her name to several biblical texts that refer to an unnamed woman. In the verses of chapter seven immediately preceding Luke's listing of the women who supported Jesus, there is a story of an unnamed woman who is a "sinner" (Luke 7:37), and the use of that word to describe a woman has throughout the ages been deemed a description of her *sexual* character, despite the fact that the precise sinful activity is never identified. Bible commentators seem to express a wide range of views about whether Mary Magdalene is described in the Luke 7:36–50 scenario, but a number of scholars, and certainly more contemporary scholars, have acknowledged that Mary Magdalene should be considered separate and apart from the unnamed woman.

This story of the woman with the bad name, the alabaster jar, the loose hair, the "many sins," the stricken conscience, the ointment, the rubbing of feet, and the kissing of feet would, over time, become the dramatic high point of the story of Mary Magdalene. The scene would be explicitly attached to her, and rendered again and again by the greatest Christian artists. But even a casual reading of this text, however charged its juxtaposition with the subsequent verses, suggests that the two women have nothing to do with each other—that the weeping anointer is no more connected to Mary of Magdala than she is to Joanna or Susanna.[2]

This notion of the sexual impurity of Mary Magdalene, follower of Jesus Christ, seems to have been understood more widely as some sort of stamp of evil applicable perhaps to other women. "She symbolizes the belief that women . . . are ultimately a symbol of evil, and of dependent sinful humanity."[3]

Yes, she was delivered of seven demons but in the biblical record of the deliverance ministry of Jesus Christ there are no stories of Jesus casting out the demon of sexual immorality. This, of course, is the problem with the mischaracterization of Mary Magdalene, a follower, financial supporter, and messenger of Jesus Christ (Matthew 28:10; John 20:17). That wrong characterization makes it easier to see *other* women followers through the lens of sexuality rather than humanity, or gender rather than contribution, or personality rather than spirituality. How many women have become the object of human limitation rather than the subject of the Lord's liberation?

Nonetheless, at the end it is Mary Magdalene and other women who stood at the crucifixion while the last life ebbed from Jesus's tortured body. And it is Mary Magdalene who came to the tomb on that Sunday morning to anoint Jesus's body for burial. And it is Mary Magdalene who encountered the risen Savior and carried the message of Christ's resurrection to the disciples. Can she be considered anything less than a disciple?

Duc In Altum. There is a chapel in Magdala, the home of Mary Magdalene. It sits on the edge of the Sea of Galilee. Its Latin name, *Duc In Altum* (meaning "launch into the deep") comes from Scripture: "When he had finished speaking, he said to Simon, 'Put out into deep water, and let down the nets for a catch'" (Luke 5:4). As the excavation took place in the early 2000s for the building of what was to be a Catholic retreat center, the ruins of an ancient synagogue were discovered, dating back to the time of Jesus Christ. It is believed that perhaps Mary Magdalene may have been in this very location.

This elegant white stone chapel does not honor Mary of Magdala alone. The first space encountered as one enters the building is the Women's Atrium, an octagonal-shaped hall with eight pillars, each named after the women followers and supporters of Jesus Christ. The women from Luke 8:2–3 are included as are Mary and her sister Martha; Salome, the mother of James and John; the mother-in-law of Simon Peter; Mary, the wife of Cleopas; and many other women as listed in Mark 15:41.

The biblical record provides very little detail about the lives of these women. Many of them are mentioned by name only once or twice. Some of them are never mentioned by name yet they are pillars, supporting the ministry of Jesus in ways far richer than what appears on the surface.

Mary Magdalene—follower of Jesus and present at His crucifixion, as explained.

Susanna, and Joanna, the wife of Chuza—followers of Jesus (Luke 8:3). They are listed in the group of women described as having been healed from evil spirits or diseases. But the woman Joanna deserves an even closer look. She is casually mentioned as "the wife of Chuza." But who was Chuza? He was a "steward" to Herod Antipas, a Jewish ruler appointed by the colonizing state of Rome to lead Judea and ensure that the Jewish people there continued to pay taxes and tribute to the enrichment of the Roman Empire. Antipas was the leader who divorced one wife and married the wife of his half brother, an act that came under the severe critique of John the Baptist. Antipas was the son of King Herod, who ordered the death of all Hebrew children under the age of two years old when he was informed by wise men of the pending birth of the One who they called "King of the Jews"—prophetically predicting the birth of Jesus Christ.

Think about the courage it took for this woman, Joanna, to not only follow, but financially support Jesus, given her husband's position under a leader who was diametrically opposed to this new movement that John the Baptist had prepared for and that Jesus Christ had inaugurated. The kingdom Jesus represented would be quite different from the kingdom that had evolved under the Herodian dynasty. Tradition also suggests that Joanna was the "Junia" mentioned in Paul's letter to the Romans: "Greet Andronicus and Junia, my fellow Jews who have been in prison with me. They are outstanding among the apostles, and they were in Christ before I was" (Romans 16:7).

Note that she is described as an "apostle."

Mary and her sister Martha—followers of Jesus (Luke 10:38–39). These two women make us smile. They both clearly loved Jesus, but showed it in very different ways. Mary was a reflective woman who was thirsty for knowledge, and she sat at the feet of Jesus; while Martha was more of what we might today call a type A personality who wants to act to serve.

> As Jesus and his disciples were on their way, he came to a village where a woman named Martha opened her home to him. She had a sister called Mary, who sat at the Lord's feet listening to what he said. But Martha was distracted by all the preparations that had to be made. She came to him and asked, "Lord, don't you care that my sister has left me to do the work by myself? Tell her to help me!" (Luke 10:38–40)

Salome, the mother of James and John—supporter of Jesus and wife of Zebedee (Matthew 20:20); she was present at the crucifixion and at Jesus's tomb. This Salome is different from the one who danced before Herod Antipas. Prompted by her mother Herodias, that Salome asked for the head of John the Baptist on a platter. This Salome was the mother of two of Jesus's disciples, the brothers James and John, mentioned as the "sons of thunder" who wanted to "call fire down from heaven to destroy" the inhabitants of Samaria who objected to providing accommodations for Jesus as He traveled to Jerusalem (Luke 9:54).

Simon Peter's mother-in-law—healed by Jesus, then supporter of Jesus (Matthew 8:14–15).

Simon, who is later named Peter, had a mother-in-law whom

the Jewish historian Josephus identified as "Graphys," indicating that she was in the lineage of the Herodian leaders of Judea. God's Word is careful to point out that she, in gratitude, cooked a meal for Jesus after He healed her. Family is not always blood. It can also be spirit.

Mary, wife of Clopas—follower of Jesus and present at His crucifixion (John 19:25).

Many other women—the many women who followed and supported Jesus (Mark 15:41).

These women were sacrificial servers who took risks to follow a man who was at once popular and unpopular, who threatened and was deemed a threat by those in power, and who carried in His body and spirit a message that was irresistible to those who ultimately committed to Him: that God in Christ was, reconciling the world to himself, and that those who received that message would themselves become reconcilers and ambassadors, pointing the way back to a right relationship with God and right relationships with people.

The task of supporting the ministry of the church is all too familiar for African American women of faith. Historically Black Christian women have served their churches in every possible way. Even when preaching women were few and far between, women taught Sunday school, served in the kitchen, organized fundraisers, kept the church clean, prayed into the wee hours of the night, gave generously, sang in the choir and played the piano, worked in the office and kept the books, took care of the pastor, visited the sick and shut-in, gave food to the hungry, and welcomed the stranger; and that was not all. Much of this work was unheralded, underappreciated, and underestimated, although absolutely essential to the survival of the church, then and now.

Pillars also stand in society. They stand for Jesus in myriad ways, contributing to the world their skills and gifting, their prayers, their dreams—*and* their faith. It is this faith expressed through extraordinary lives that is so often overlooked, underappreciated, or simply ignored. The truth is that faith in Jesus Christ has been the source of strength, courage, and ingenuity, the secret fuel to the engines of their lives. If we would only look, we would find faith holding up, supporting these pillars that support the church.

Pillars of Society; Pillars of Faith

Pillars also stand in our society today. They stand for Jesus in many ways, contributing to the world their skills and gifting, their prayers, their dreams, and their faith. Their faith expressed through extraordinary living is also often overlooked, under-appreciated, and simply ignored. The truth is that faith in Jesus Christ has been the source of their strength, courage, ingenuity, the secret fuel to the engines of their lives too. If we take a closer look we will see that it is faith in Jesus that causes these pillars to stand.

Katherine Johnson—mathematician

A true pioneer, Katherine Goble Johnson was made famous by the film, "Hidden Figures," which tells the truth about the female African American mathematicians who performed the complex calculations underlying the engineering of the NASA space program. The film is based on the book *Hidden Figures: The American Dream and the Untold Story of the Black Women Mathematicians Who Helped Win the Space Race* by Margot Lee Shetterly, an African American woman. Unknown to most of us, a group of highly intelligent Black women, together with White women, were the first "computers," performing highly advanced equations by hand. The film highlights the lives of three women, Katherine Johnson, mathematician; Mary Jackson, engineer; and Dorothy Vaughan, mathematician and Fortran expert. Katherine Johnson garners a great deal of the film's attention because of her outstanding math skills and her ability to envision the equations essential to the accomplishment of never-done-before aeronautical feats of space travel. Her precision is lauded in the film as being comparable to the accuracy of the early computers first used by NASA.

In fact, John Glenn wants "the girl" to check the computer's calculations prior to liftoff. When Al Harrison clarifies whether Glenn is referring to Katherine, Glenn replies in the affirmative: "And if she says they're good, I'm ready to go."[4]

John Glenn, the astronaut, is about to make history and not surprisingly wants to have confidence in the mathematical calculations underlying his journey, so he turns to the intelligence demonstrated by Katherine Johnson, whose skill and ingenuity are key to the space program. Katherine is asked to fact-check the computer's analysis because Glenn and others had greater trust in people than machines at that point in history.

In the film version, in the few moments before takeoff, Glenn makes his request that Katherine check the numbers, which she does as all eyes watch the launch, in an apparent delay to the start of the countdown. In fact, what is portrayed in the film as a series of calculations that took minutes, actually took a day and a half.[5] Nonetheless, Katherine concludes that the computer's numbers are accurate because they match her own!

The genius of Katherine Johnson is clearly on display, but is it possible that her faith was a factor in her success? Should we not also highlight her longtime membership in church, that she is a faithful member of the choir, that she is a praying woman? Author Shetterly refers to "providence" as the reason Katherine was the person selected to analyze the calculations.[6] There was an unseen hand in the orchestration of these events, but not an unknown one. It seems that Katherine's ability to produce never-seen-before calculations for never-seen-before scientific achievements was in all likelihood related to her faith in an unseen yet powerfully present God. A person who was trained by her faith to know that *unseen* does not mean *unreal* or that "impossible" might actually be at home in the realm of invention.

It is noteworthy that this woman of faith became a real pillar in America's space program at a crucial time in its development, when the lives of precious astronauts depended on accurate hypotheses for their very lives. Katherine Goble Johnson became a living example of walking by faith and not by sight.

Mary McLeod Bethune—educator and government official

Mary McLeod Bethune started the Daytona Educational and Industrial Training School for Negro Girls with items gathered from the city dump and trash piles behind hotels—her teacher's desk was a packing crate. They mashed elderberries for ink and used charred splinters of wood for pencils, so she was no stranger to God's miraculous provision.[7] But facing the Ku Klux Klan in the nighttime darkness would require a demonstration of faith and courage. She could see the lights in the distance. Indeed, the Klan was approaching the school. Mary McLeod Bethune had a plan. As the white robes approached, Mrs. Bethune told the teachers to turn on all the outdoor campus lights. Then she simply took her stand, head held high, as the procession of Klan members moved through the area campus and exited on the other side of the quadrangle.[8]

Some versions of this event assert that she and her students sang spirituals to turn away the notorious night riders but one thing is certain: Mary McLeod Bethune stood on her faith in founding the school in Daytona, Florida, and she would continue to do so as the school grew and flourished.[9]

The night riders appeared on campus in response to Mary Bethune's voter's registration activity. As soon as women gained the right to vote, she became actively involved in preparing Black women and men to register, pay the poll tax, and vote. In 1920 and in 1922, the school faced the threat of Klan violence on the campus but Mary McLeod Bethune was resolute. The day after the Klan marched through the campus, she joined one hundred other Black citizens in exercising the right to vote in the 1922 mayoral election.

The life of this great woman of faith involves the succession of one miraculous achievement after another. Born to a mother who had been enslaved, Mary was the fifteenth of seventeen children but somehow was sent off to gain an education, ultimately becoming the only Black student at Dwight L. Moody's Institute for Home and Foreign Mission, in Chicago.[10] When her application for missionary service was turned down by the Presbyterian Church, she turned her efforts to the field of education. She started the Daytona all-girls boarding school in 1904 that later merged with Cookman Institute for boys. Bethune-Cookman college became an accredited four-year college in 1931 and was finally named Bethune-Cookman University in 2007. Despite the fact that Mary didn't learn to read until she was eleven years old, she became the first African American female college president at the school she started in a rented room.

She would go on to become the president of the National Association of Colored Women, and then later formed the National Council of Negro Women. She championed the right of women to vote, and served in the cabinet of President Franklin Delano Roosevelt as the head of the Federal Youth Administration. She became friends with First Lady Eleanor Roosevelt and through this relationship, funding was set aside to train Black aviators, developing the pilots who would eventually become the Tuskegee Airmen. Mary McLeod Bethune's life was one of extraordinary impact and extraordinary faith.

In her *My Last Last Will and Testament*, written in 1954, one year before she passed away, Mary McLeod Bethune shared wisdom and life lessons as though she were giving gifts to loved ones in a will. Speaking to her "heirs," the community at large, Mary McLeod Bethune did not leave silver or gold but rather "love and hope." She did not leave buildings or bank accounts; rather, she left the challenge of developing "confidence in one another" and a thirst for education. Mrs. Bethune included in her bequest respect for power and racial dignity, harmonious living, and care for young people. Yet her legacy is completed with the gift of faith.

> I Leave You Faith. Faith is the first factor in a life devoted to service. Without faith, nothing is possible. With it, nothing is impossible. Faith in God is the greatest power, but great, too, is faith in oneself.[11]

She was not a preacher. She did not take the title of *Reverend*, but her faith was the unmistakable ground of her being. As her life is remembered and celebrated, the power she accessed through her belief and trust in God cannot be overlooked but is an integral part of the significant role she played in education and government.

Harriet Powers—artist

Stories can be told in so many different ways. Through song and art and dance and prose. Quilts tell stories, too, and Harriet Powers, born a slave in Athens, Georgia, in 1837, is widely regarded as the forerunner of the African American story quilt tradition.[12] Her two remaining quilts are displayed in the Museum of Fine Arts in Boston, Massachusetts, and the Smithsonian Institute.

In 1886 a trained artist spotted a highly unique quilt at a county fair. The "Bible Quilt" featured eleven panels, each depicting a story from the Bible. The creator of the quilt was a married mother of nine, Harriet Powers. At first Harriet refused to sell the quilt to the zealous would-be purchaser but when hard times hit the Powers family, she and her husband made the difficult decision to sell it to Jennie Smith for five dollars, which was half of their original asking price. Jennie Smith knew immediately that this quilt was perhaps the first of its kind, because it told a story.

Quilting in the African American community is connected to the appliqué wall-hanging tradition of Central and West African countries, often telling the stories of kings.[13] Enslaved women carried the tradition of their native lands with them to the Americas, and developed a vibrant practice combining American folk-quilt traditions with their own. Story quilts can be a powerful visual message of a personal or community event, family history—or instructions for a plantation escape. Harriet Powers expressed her faith in her quilts.

Even though Harriet was compelled by financial circumstances to sell her quilt, she refused to do so without explaining each of the panels. First, she had to tell the story. She began with Adam and Eve in the garden of Eden, then she explained further a continuance of paradise with Eve and a son; Satan amidst the seven stars; Cain killing his brother Abel, and going into the land of Nod to get a wife; Jacob's dream; the baptism of Christ; the crucifixion; Judas Iscariot and the thirty pieces of silver, and the Last Supper; and the holy family. She did not just explain her artistry, she was telling the Bible in story form.

A story quilt draws us into the events, gives us visual cues, and releases our imagination. Her pictorial quilts feature biblical scenes but also include local events like the 1833 meteor shower. In her words, "The falling of the stars on Nov. 13, 1833. The people were frightened and thought that the end had come. God's hand staid the stars. The varmints rushed out of their beds."[14] Her quilts invite all who view them to tell and retell the stories of life and the stories of faith.

Generations later, the stories of faith that Harriet Powers loved still speak through her quilts. They speak to us without the limitation of words. They speak to us without the limitation of voice. They call to our spirits with vibrant pattern and color, stirring us to visualize a living spiritual reality.

Mahalia Jackson—culture influencer

"Tell them about the dream." These few words encouraged Rev. Dr. Martin Luther King Jr. to stop reading his notes and speak from his heart at the historic 1963 March on Washington. Mahalia Jackson spoke those words and Dr. King heeded her voice and proceeded to give one of the most powerful and memorable speeches in modern times. Her voice, among the crowd gathered around him on the steps of the Lincoln Memorial, would have been familiar to Dr. King. It was a voice he'd heard in some of his most trying moments singing gospel songs of the Baptist Church to him through the phone.

Mahalia Jackson was an amazing singer and she was so much more. Born in New Orleans in 1911, she was raised in a strict Baptist household with extended family and siblings after her mother died when she was five years old. She was exposed as a youngster to traditional Baptist singing, but she enjoyed listening to the very spirited music of the Pentecostal church near her home. Fascinated by singing at an early age, Mahalia developed a strong voice and singing presence that was a combination of several musical styles she enjoyed, including popular blues singers Bessie Smith and Ma Rainey.

Singing from the age of four years, Mahalia became a gifted church musician as one of the Johnson Singers and also as a soloist. It would be some time, however, before she would earn income from her singing because the commercial gospel music industry did not really exist when she released her first recording in 1937.[15] Her label, Decca Records, tried to get her to sing secular music but she refused. She was determined to keep her vow to God that she would not sing secular music. Her 1948 recording of "Move On Up A Little Higher" on Apollo Records catapulted her onto the national music scene, selling more than one million records.[16] That was just the beginning.

Somehow, the gospel-music-only Mahalia Jackson achieved a level of success and popularity equal to or greater than that of her secular counterparts. When she appeared on the extremely popular *Ed Sullivan Show* in 1956, Mahalia sung "with the power that had wrecked churches in Chicago" according to Anthony Heilbut, noted critic and historian displaying a kind of singing witnessed rarely, if ever, outside of the sacred sanctuary.[17] But that was Mahalia Jackson, powerful gospeler and popular household-name singer. Materials published for a New Orleans celebration of her life depicted her as "the most powerful voice in the history of sacred music in America."[18]

Mahalia Jackson would go on to record albums for Columbia Records, sing at the inauguration of John F. Kennedy and at his funeral, appear in the film "Imitation of Life," and join Duke Ellington at the Newport Jazz Festival. Her fame, however, not only served to bolster her musical career, but it also bolstered the Civil Rights Movement. Mahalia was asked on several occasions to support the movement by holding concerts and donating proceeds. Rev. Ralph Abernathy introduced her to Dr. Martin Luther King Jr. and a friendship developed that Dr. King would turn to in some of his darkest moments.

On numerous occasions, Ms. Jackson was asked to lend her voice to the secular world of music but she stood her ground, laying the foundation for a career in singing the Gospel of Jesus Christ that lifted her to heights she likely would have never reached otherwise. Her determination to stay on the gospel road that God had placed her on took her on a journey that reached Germany, France, Norway, India, Japan, and the continent of Africa.[19]

The door she closed led her to the door that God opened, through which her amazing grace-filled voice was clearly heard.

Cathy Hughes—media mogul

At home in Omaha, Nebraska, she knew. From a very young age she knew. Cathy Hughes knew she wanted to be in radio. "Nothing gave me more inspiration, nothing gave me more stimulation—I almost didn't complete grade school and junior high school because all I was thinking about was my future in radio. It just overtook my entire spirit."[20] Her path, however, was not exactly linear.

After moving to Washington, DC, to start her professional career in media, she landed a job at Howard University's radio station, WHUR. Eventually she became the first Black female vice president and general manager of a radio station. Her dream was bigger than working at a station; she dreamed of owning one and it would take extreme faith to continue to believe in her dream after being turned down by thirty-two lending institutions. Finally, on the thirty-third try, a female Puerto Rican loan officer said yes.

Her dream became reality when she purchased WOL-AM radio. The dream was costly. Depleted of her other assets, Cathy and her son Alfred Liggins III found themselves sleeping on the floor of the station but her faith continued to sustain her. She resisted the pressure to give up her lifelong quest when her mother suggested she find a more reliable government position. She weathered the storms and the station became a success and launched her pioneering career in media leadership and ownership.

Her achievements over the years have continued to mount as the acquisition of one radio station has morphed into a multimedia conglomerate including radio stations, television, print media, and digital platforms. Urban One is one of the largest diversified media companies in the US that targets primarily an African American audience. And the little boy who had to sleep with her on the floor of that first radio station became the CEO of Urban One. Cathy Hughes was the first African American female chair of a publicly traded corporation.[21] She has been inducted into the Radio Hall of Fame, The Black History Hall of Fame, and the Cable Hall of Fame, but perhaps her most fruitful affiliation is not with the famous but with the faithful.

> I believe you should pray as hard on those up days as you do on the down days. That's the reason I believe in the power of prayer because I believe you have to be able to first believe in a being superior to you. . . . You have to believe in God and once you're able to believe in God and embrace the greatness of the creator, then you're able to believe in yourself and embrace the greatness that God put into you and each of us, and you're able to tap into that. But there will be days.[22]

Hughes's faith has carried her through all of her days.

Gabrielle Douglas—athlete and mentor

Gabrielle Douglas certainly took a leap of faith into the world of gymnastics; that is how she tells her story. In 2012, she became the first African American woman and first woman of color of any nationality to win Olympic Gold as an individual All-Around Gold Medalist. Gabrielle points to her faith and the faith of her family in her biography, *Grace, Gold, and Glory: My Leap of Faith*. "With strong faith in God and some serious determination, every dream is possible—especially if your mama refuses to let you fly home, fry chicken, and give up."[23] With wit and candor Gabrielle Douglas tells her pioneering story of training for the Olympics as well as growing up in the Douglas family with two parents who were part of the Word of Faith movement in Tulsa, Oklahoma.

She tells of her rocky beginnings as a baby living with her family in the back of a Dodge van and the employment and financial challenges that almost threatened to rob her of an opportunity to put her natural athletic ability to use as a gymnast. Money and employment were not the only obstacles to her future in gymnastics. As an infant she was diagnosed with a life-threatening blood disorder and like many other families struggling with poverty, doctors' care was not affordable. Gabby Douglas's mother literally prayed her daughter back to health. From that time Gabby Douglas has enjoyed excellent health, another factor Gabby attributes to God.

Gabrielle believes that God was directing her path all along, guiding her into the Olympic arena. Repeatedly throughout her story she highlights the hand of God. "I don't believe in coincidence. So when I look back on all the experiences that led to my first day at Gymstrada, I can definitely see how the Lord put me on the path that He designed for me."[24]

This heralding of God as the source of her strength is markedly different from the accounts so often given of success as being the result of strong will and determination. What happens, though, when human strength runs dry and the well of determination is empty? This is the territory of faith. Just a few months before her historic win, Gabrielle wanted to give up her gymnastics quest but for reasons she ascribes to faith, Gabrielle pushed and pressed and became a record-setting champion.

Her story in book form has become a wonderful lesson for young people about the power of faith, and her story has also become the subject of the 2014 Lifetime film, "The Gabby Douglas Story." God took a homeless, sickly infant and transformed her into a champion athlete on the world stage whose story is told in print and on film. As Gabrielle stood on the gold medal podium at the 2012 Olympics in London, England, she remembered "that day seven months earlier when I almost gave up on my goal. In an instant, all the sacrifices, the injuries, and the homesickness felt worth it. On August 2, 2012, my leap of faith became God's gracious gift to me."[25]

With the exception of those who have read her book or perhaps viewed her movie, very few people may be aware of the faith that fueled every moment of her life, and her training and preparation for her gymnastics career. Gabrielle, however, speaks of her life and dependence on God with sincerity and conviction, pointing to prayers and not prowess, faith and not luck, collective support and not individual achievement, and to a loving and always-present God.

Latasha Morrison—reconciler

How can we talk to one another across ethnic divides and beyond the stereotypes that haunt us? That is the question that Latasha Morrison sought to answer—and it pointed her to the church. She discovered that although the Christian faith did have answers, the church itself was a poor witness. "The longer I worked in the church, the more I came to see that it wasn't a credible witness for racial reconciliation."[26] So Latasha started her own conversations. She learned what she may have known instinctively: that her White friends knew very little about the Black experience. So she started with the film *The Color Purple*, the coming-of-age story from the book of the same title by Alice Walker, about an abused Black girl. An informal movie discussion turned into a racial reconciliation discussion group that met monthly. When Ferguson, Missouri, erupted after the shooting death of Michael Brown by a police officer, the conversations turned to that national tragedy.

> Attending the monthly circles ensured they wouldn't remain silent, wouldn't be complicit.

> As they became aware of racial injustice and the
> history of discrimination, it became impossible
> for them to turn a blind eye.[27]

It wasn't just a discussion of current events, though. Latasha's friends lacked the historical context to understand the significance of the contemporary experiences of African Americans. And African Americans, Morrison discovered, lacked the courageous and honest conversations with their Anglo counterparts. Latasha was compelled to share the history of injustice facing African Americans and to challenge her friends to look deep within to examine their own complicity.[28] Raw, tearful, and painful conversations happened, and the people in Latasha's group kept talking. That's half the battle.

What if we applied the Gospel to solving the ills of society?

Centered on three main areas of interaction, Latasha's book, *Be the Bridge*, outlines a way to build a bridge based on the Gospel of Jesus Christ: the bridge to lament, the bridge to confession and repentance, and the bridge to restorative reconciliation. The book introduces a methodology based on Christian practice and tradition, prayer, and reflection that invite the Holy Spirit into the conversations. *Be the Bridge* groups have formed all over the United States, coming together to build bridges rooted in faith and in the love of a living God who calls us to be family. Morrison reminds us of God's invitation: "God is inviting all of us to be active participants in racial reconciliation, to show the world that racial unity is possible through Christ."[29]

Despite the pain of the process, the overwhelming breadth of our racial divide, and the sheer gravity of the state of relations between racial-ethnic groups in this country, Latasha has witnessed cold hearts warm up and blind eyes open.[30]

The church is, after all, not a building. It is not a location. It is a set of relationships with God, with friends, and with enemies. The church should demonstrate to the world that Jesus Christ is alive. What if we applied the Gospel to solving the ills of society? What if we actively looked for the pattern, the shape of love drawn for us in the Bible, and commenced to build it just the way God said? What if we all took seriously this assignment to become bridges? Bridges need pillars to support the weight of the bridge and the precious cargo crossing.

The Eighth Pillar

There is one more pillar in the Women's Atrium at Duc In Altum. It is an unmarked pillar. Female visitors to the chapel are told to trace their names into the marble, adding their story to the stories of countless women who love Jesus in their living, who stand and pray and work, spreading the Gospel to all generations.

EPILOGUE

There is an amazing scene in the movie *Beloved*, based on the book by the late, brilliant Nobel Prize–winning author Toni Morrison. The book revolves around an enslaved woman, Sethe, who has been brutalized physically and sexually by her captors and her captors' children for many years. When her children are very young, she decides to try to escape with them and is caught. Rather than have her children experience the horrors she has been subjected to, she makes an anguished decision to kill them on the spot. She is only able to kill one, a daughter, whom she later names Beloved. Her actions scream out to us over the centuries the unbearable nature of the "peculiar institution" of chattel slavery.

The book and the movie play out the psycho-spiritual consequences of Sethe's decision in many ways, but one of the ways is that her dead daughter comes back to haunt her, in a very real, visual, sensory way. Beloved "comes back" as a grown young woman with a scar on her neck—evidence of her mother's shame—and proceeds to wreak havoc on her mother's life.

But there is a group of amazing Christian women who recognize the spiritual attack on Sethe. The devil comes to steal, kill, and destroy (see John 10:10), but they decide to take that devil on.

Sethe's daughter—the one she didn't kill—is on the front porch when the women come. One starts to sing: "I heard the voice," she begins. "I heeaarrd the voice," she is singing and wailing. The others are crying out too. Then they start to sing in harmony. The elders call it "lining a hymn": "of Jesus say, come unto me and rest." One continues, "Lay down my weary one, lay down thy head upon my breast." The others follow in harmony. Sethe comes out with the demon. Her eyes are wet with tears. She thinks she sees her enslaver and goes after the apparition. The women surround her, raising their hands and crying out. Finally the demon just disappears into thin air.[1]

It is finished. The exorcism is complete.

The women in *A Cloud of Women*, whether they are also described in the Bible or annotated in our history, are these women who have slain dragons and devils. They have pulled people from the brink, they have changed societies and cultures and systems, and they have spoken truth to power. They have been emotionally shipwrecked and attacked from without and within. They have been "'buked, and scorned, and talked about," as the old folks say.

Yet they persisted. Yet they continued to do what they were called to do. They prayed through and cried through. They fought. Weary or energized, joyful or sorrowful, they fought all the way through.

Their stories are our stories. We can take comfort in the fact that we are not alone.

They are your ancestors, you know
By birth, by blood, by culture, by faith
Hailing from Africa and the ancient gardens of
Mesopotamia
Hailing from a faith that would not fail
A faith that moved the hearts of kings, of spouses,
of sisters, of children,
of God.
And now, they are your witnesses
Witnesses of an earlier time
And witnesses of you now,
A mighty cloud
Urging you to go on, go on.
Here is what they say:
We are women
We too are made in the image of God

Male and female created He them.
We can be wisdom,
Calling from the heights of the city
Inviting those who know not
to eat the bread and drink the wine
and proceed in the way of understanding.
We can be the mother hen
who gathers the brood under her wing
and provides shelter and comfort.
We can speak blessing
and become the vessel
through which others' years are multiplied.
Learn from them as you create your own stories,
and then tell them to your children and grandchil-
dren, so that the story can continue.

A Cloud of Women play

ACKNOWLEDGMENTS

This journey began when Sis. Mary White, First Lady of my former church, Mt. Lebanon-Strathmoor in Detroit, invited me to do a presentation for Women's Day. She gave me carte blanche and trusted me, and that was the beginning of my play *A Cloud of Women*. When I joined my present church, Plymouth United Church of Christ in Detroit, my cowriter and then–Associate Minister Rev. Dr. Georgia Hill invited me to do an expanded version for our Women's Retreat; and then my current Senior Pastor, Rev. Dr. Nicholas Hood III, invited me to produce it for a church service. So many others to thank! Former Michigan State Representative Leslie Love, who directed the theater program at Marygrove College and shepherded the play's first professional production; the late, wonderful Sandra D. Hines, who was my second professional director and put her own genius spin on it; my friend Judi Caliman and Director Debra Carter, who brought the play to Tabernacle Missionary Baptist Church; my mother-in-law Jessie Reeder, who invited me to do the play at our annual United Conference for Women, expanding the play to Ohio; brilliant Director Timothy Cross, who expanded the play into several theaters in Illinois; the churches that have done the play over the years; and the many wonderful actors who have embodied these roles so passionately, including my own mother, who played Sarah in the first full version. She truly embodies Sarah's words, "I can smile about it now." Of course, I would not even be at this table without the referral of my good friend, mentor, and colleague Matthew Parker. Finally, I owe a deep debt of gratitude to my editor Joyce

Dinkins and Our Daily Bread Publishing's VOICES Collection for working with Rev. Georgia and me to shape this book and bring it to life. It is a joy to work with such thoughtful, brilliant women!
—Diane Proctor Reeder

My grandmother was a church lady. For Easter one year Mom made my sister and me matching yellow coats which we wore to attend church with Grandmother at Mother Bethel AME in Philadelphia, Pennsylvania. Complete with white gloves, church hat, and peppermints, Mary Johnson was a picture of faith. She and my mother, Valentine Hill, were the first women of faith I witnessed, and their lives of quiet prayer, devotion to family, and trust in the Lord set the bar. I am so grateful to them and to the circle of faithful women who did and still do pray for, encourage, counsel, and chide me. Without this cloud of witnesses, especially the 7:00 a.m. Women's Prayer Line, this book would not exist.

Thank you, Diane Reeder, coauthor and friend, for the grace you so readily offer and the skill you generously share. Thank you, Joyce Dinkins, our editor, for the intelligence and gifting shaped by your faith that shepherded us through this process with great love. Working with Our Daily Bread Publishing has been a joy.

To Janet Hill Talbert and Ellen Hill Zeringue, my sisters, there is not room here to thank you for the love that we share. You two have been nothing less than extraordinary blessings in my life. You always hold up my hands during the fight.

I can still see my father's broad smile that encouraged me countless times in ministry and in life. In memory of Dr. George C. Hill, I hope this book brings smiles to its readers. My grandfather, Ishmael R. Johnson, and my uncles, Robert Johnson and the late Barry Johnson, continued to assure me that effort would be rewarded with results.

I am grateful to Matthew Parker, whose considerable influence and power of connection made this book opportunity possible—and for making room within his networks for women in ministry.

To all the women and men, in the pew and the pulpit, who mentored, challenged, and nurtured me in the faith, I say Thank

You! To my late aunts, Ruth Johnson, Exhorter, and the Rev. Mrs. L. A. Moore, amazing women of faith, I say Thank You! To the Only Wise God, I say Thank You!

—Georgia A. Hill

NOTES

Introduction

1. "In 'Color of the Cross,' Jesus Is Black," Today, October 25, 2006, https://www.today.com/popculture/color-cross-jesus -black-wbna15415921.
2. Georgina Lawton, "How Unconscious Biases Affect Black Women Today," *Bustle*, February 16, 2017, https://www.bustle .com/p/7-unconscious-biases-that-still-affect-black-women -today-36379.
3. Prathia Hall, *Beyond Eden: The Collected Sermons and Essays of Prathia Hall*, ed. Courtney Pace (Atlanta: University of Georgia Press, 2022), 189–91.

Chapter 1

1. Madeleine L'Engle, *And It Was Good: Reflections on Beginnings* (Colorado Springs, CO: Convergent Books, 2017; Wheaton, IL: Harold Shaw Publishers, 1983), Locations #58–59, 62–64, Kindle edition.
2. Erin Blakemore, "How the Daughter of a Slave Became the First African-American Woman to Earn a Bachelor's Degree," *Time*, May 23, 2017, https://time.com/4788672/mary-jane -patterson-history/.
3. Jackson Landers, "Unbought and Unbossed: When a Black Woman Ran for the White House," *Smithsonian*, April 25, 2016, https://www.smithsonianmag.com/smithsonian-institution /unbought-and unbossed-when-black-woman-ran-for-the-white -house-180958699/.
4. Lakesia Collins, as quoted in Chima Akiro, "Being the First Black Woman: A Blessing and a Curse," *South Side Weekly*, April 21, 2022, https://southsideweekly.com/being-the-first -black-woman-a-blessing-and-a-curse/.

Chapter 2

1. Robin Gallaher Branch, "Deborah in the Bible," Biblical Archaeology Society, November 8, 2022, https://www .biblicalarchaeology.org/daily/people-cultures-in-the-bible /people-in-the-bible/deborah-in-the-bible/.
2. Martin Luther King Jr., "I Have a Dream," as quoted in Ashely K. Speed, "Remembering Dr. Martin Luther King Jr.," William & Mary University Advancement, January 16, 2017, https:// advancement.wm.edu/news/2017/remembering-dr--martin-luther -king-jr-.php.
3. Hortense Powdermaker, *After Freedom: A Cultural Study in the Deep South*, as quoted in Maegan Parker Brooks, *A Voice That Could Stir an Army* (Jackson: University of Mississippi Press, 2014), as analyzed in Charles M. Payne, *I've Got the Light of Freedom: The Organizing Tradition and the Mississippi Freedom Struggle* (Berkeley: University of California Press, 1995), 23.
4. Maegan Parker Brooks, *A Voice That Could Stir an Army: Fannie Lou Hamer and the Rhetoric of the Black Freedom Movement* (Jackson: University of Mississippi Press, 2014), Location #17, Kindle edition.
5. Parker Brooks, *A Voice That Could Stir an Army*, Location #27, Kindle edition.
6. Parker Brooks, *A Voice That Could Stir an Army*, Location #18, Kindle edition.
7. Maegan Parker Brooks and Davis W. Houck, eds., *The Speeches of Fannie Lou Hamer: To Tell It Like It Is* (Jackson: University of Mississippi Press, 2013), Locations #3–4, Kindle edition.
8. Pam Otten, "Deborah: Embracing God's Call," in *She Is Called: Women of the Bible*, Faithward, accessed February 5, 2023, https://www.faithward.org/deborah-embracing-gods-call/.
9. Parker Brooks and Houck, eds., *The Speeches of Fannie Lou Hamer*, Location #5, Kindle edition.
10. Barbara Ransby, *Ella Baker and the Black Freedom Movement: A Radical Democractic Vision* (Chapel Hill, NC: University of North Carolina Press), 364.
11. Parker Brooks and Houck, eds., *The Speeches of Fannie Lou Hamer*, Location #445, Kindle edition.
12. Franklyn Peterson, "Sunflowers Don't Grow in Sunflower County," *Sepia* 19 (1970): 17.
13. Parker Brooks, *A Voice That Could Stir an Army*, Location #39, Kindle edition.
14. Parker Brooks, *A Voice That Could Stir an Army*, Location #11, Kindle edition.
15. Interview by the author with Denise Page Hood, October 3, 2022.

16. Diane Bukowski, "Shocking New Details Emerge in Godboldo Police Stand-Off Case," *Voice of Detroit*, July 27, 2011, https://voiceofdetroit.net/2011/07/27/shocking-new-details-in-godboldo-police-stand-off-case.
17. Doug Guthrie, "Detroit Mother Jailed after Standoff," *Detroit News*, March 28, 2011.
18. Ed White, "Lawyers Who Challenged Michigan's 2020 Election Results Penalized," *Christian Science Monitor*, August 16, 2021, https://www.csmonitor.com/USA/Justice/2021/0826/Lawyers-who-challenged-Michigan-s-2020-election-results-penalized.
19. "Descendant of Racial Terror Lynching Victim Joins Michigan Supreme Court," Equal Justice Initiative, January 3, 2023, https://eji.org/news/descendant-of-racial-terror-lynching-victim-joins-michigan-supreme-court/.

Chapter 3

1. *Word History Encyclopedia*, s.v. "The Maccabean Revolt," by Harry Oats, October 29, 2015, https://www.worldhistory.org/article/827/the-maccabean-revolt/.
2. Obery M. Hendricks Jr., *The Politics of Jesus: Rediscovering the True Revolutionary Nature of Jesus' Teachings and How They Have Been Corrupted* (New York: Three Leaves Press, 2006), Location #729, Kindle edition.
3. Lauren Weisner, "Individual and Community Trauma: Individual Experiences in Collective Environments," Illinois Criminal Justice Information Authority, July 15, 2020, https://icjia.illinois.gov/researchhub/articles/individual-and-community-trauma-individual-experiences-in-collective-environments.
4. Anna Malaika Tubbs, *The Three Mothers: How the Mothers of Martin Luther King, Jr., Malcolm X, and James Baldwin Shaped a Nation* (New York: Flatiron Books, 2021), Location #20, Kindle edition.
5. Tubbs, *The Three Mothers*, Location #43, Kindle edition.
6. Marcus Garvey, "Marcus Garvey: 'Look for Me in the Whirlwind,' Freedom Speech circa 1924," Universal Negro Improvement Assocation and African Communities League, June 25, 2020, www.unia-aclgovernment.com/marcus-garvey-look-for-me-in-the-whirlwind-freedom-speech-circa-1924.
7. Tubbs, *The Three Mothers*, Location #93, Kindle edition.
8. Tubbs, *The Three Mothers*, Location #58, Kindle edition.
9. "Why It Happened," Digital History, accessed February 5, 2023, https://www.digitalhistory.uh.edu/disp_textbook.cfm?smtID=2&psid=3432.
10. Megan Sauter, "When Was Jesus Born—B.C. or A.D.? How the

Divide between B.C. and A.D. Was Calculated," Biblical Archaeology Society, June 8, 2023, https://www.biblicalarchaeology.org/daily/people-cultures-in-the-bible/jesus-historical-jesus/when-was-jesus-born-bc-or-ad/

11. Tubbs, *The Three Mothers*, 25.
12. James Baldwin, *The Price of the Ticket* (Boston, MA: Beacon Press, 1985), 241, 156.
13. Malcom X, as quoted in Jolie Solomon, "Overlooked No More: Louise Little, Activist and Mother of Malcolm X," *New York Times*, March 19, 2022, https://www.nytimes.com/2022/03/19/obituaries/louise-little-overlooked.html. These and other Malcolm X letters are housed at the Schomburg Center for Research in Black Culture in New York City.
14. Tubbs, *The Three Mother*, Location #43, Kindle edition.
15. Martin Luther King Jr., "Chapter 1: Early Years," Martin Luther King, Jr. Research and Education Institute, Stanford University, accessed June 23, 2022, https://kinginstitute.standford.edu/king-papers/documents?page=2. The chapter is from Martin Luther King Jr., *The Autobiography of Martin Luther King, Jr.*, ed. Clayborne Carson (New York: Warner Books, 2008).

Chapter 4

1. Sojourner Truth, "Ain't I a Woman?," speech delivered to the Women's Rights Convention in Akron, Ohio, in 1851, National Park Service, accessed February 5, 2023, https://www.nps.gov/articles/sojourner-truth.htm. First published by Sojourner Truth, "Ain't I a Woman?," ed. Frances Gage, *Independent*, April 23, 1863, per The Sojourner Truth Project, https://www.thesojournertruthproject.com/compare-the-speeches.
2. Jennifer Holladay, "Sexism in the Civil Rights Movement: A Discussion Guide," Learning for Justice, July 7, 2009, https://www.learningforjustice.org/magazine/sexism-in-the-civil-rights-movement-a-discussion-guide.
3. Renita Weems, *Battered Love: Marriage, Sex, and Violence in the Hebrew Prophets* (Minneapolis: Augsburg Fortress Publishers, 1995), 12.
4. Weems, *Battered Love*, 14.
5. Weems, *Battered Love*, Location #1292, Kindle edition.
6. "Scope of the Problem: Statistics," RAINN, accessed February 10, 2023, https://www.rainn.org/statistics/scope-problem.
7. Danielle L. McGuire, *At the Dark End of the Street: Black Women, Rape, and Resistance—a New History of the Civil Rights Movement from Rosa Parks to the Rise of Black Power* (New York: Alfred A. Knopf, 2010), Location #177, Kindle edition.

8. McGuire, *At the Dark End of the Street*, Location #174, Kindle edition.

Chapter 5

1. Robin Harris also starred in a video with the same subtitle as his famous phrase. Robin Harris, "The Robin Harris Story: We Don't Die, We Multiply" (Urban Works, 2006).
2. Marian Wright Edelman, *The Measure of Our Success: A Letter to My Children and Yours* (New York: Harper Perennial, 2015), Location #48, Kindle edition.
3. Edelman, *The Measure of Our Success*, 5–6.
4. Marian Wright Edelman, "Interview with Marian Wright Edelman," December 19, 1988, Washington University in St. Louis, transcript, http://repository.wustl.edu/concern/videos/6d570197t.
5. Edelman, "Interview with Marian Wright Edelman," transcript.
6. Ellen B. Meacham, *Delta Epiphany: Robert F. Kennedy in Mississippi* (Jackson: The University of Mississippi Press, 2018), Location #88, Kindle edition.
7. Edelman, "Interview with Marian Wright Edelman," transcript.
8. Robert Kennedy, as quoted in Arthur Meier Schlesinger Jr., *Robert Kennedy and His Times* (New York: Houghton Mifflin Harcourt, 2002), Location #795, Kindle edition.
9. Marian Wright Edelman, "Still Hungry in America," *Philadelphia Tribune,* February 21, 2012, https://www.phillytrib.com /commentary/still-hungry-in-america/article_9c268ad9-7771 -5d3a-a6f9-29f23364ec2a.html.
10. Edelman, "Interview with Marian Wright Edelman," transcript.
11. Edelman, "Interview with Marian Wright Edelman," transcript.

Chapter 6

1. Ida B. Wells, "Lynching, Our National Crime," speech to the National Negro Conference, 1909, BlackPast, transcript posted September 22, 2008, https://www.blackpast.org/african -american-history/1909-ida-b-wells-awful-slaughter/.
2. Wells, "Lynching, Our National Crime," transcript.
3. Abel Meeropol, "Strange Fruit," *The New York Teacher*, January 1937.
4. Tianna Mobley, "Ida B. Wells-Barnett: Anti-Lynching and the White House," White House Historical Association, April 9, 2021, https://www.whitehousehistory.org/ida-b-wells-barnett -anti-lynching-and-the-white house.
5. Crystal Feimster, "Ida B. Wells and the Lynching of Black Women," *New York Times*, April 28, 2018, https://www

.nytimes.com/2018/04/28/opinion/sunday/ida-b-wells-lynching
-black-women.html.

6. Feimster, "Ida B. Wells and the Lynching of Black Women."
7. Ida B. Wells-Barnett, *Southern Horrors: Lynch Law in All Its Phases* (published by author, 1892), 13.
8. Wells, "Lynching, Our National Crime," transcript.
9. Mamie Till Mobley, "'Let The People See': It Took Courage To Keep Emmet Till's Memory Alive," NPR, October 30, 2018, https://www.npr.org/2018/10/30/660980178/-let-the-people-see -shows-how-emmett-till-s-murder-was-nearly-forgotten.
10. Sybrina Fulton, *Trayvon: Ten Years Later* (Amazon Original Stories, 2022), Kindle.
11. Fulton, *Trayvon: Ten Years Later*.
12. Mobley, "Ida B. Wells-Barnett: Anti-Lynching and the White House."
13. Fulton, *Trayvon: Ten Years Later*.
14. "Lucy McBath Official Biography," United States House of Representatives, accessed July 28, 2023, https://mcbath.house.gov /official-biography.
15. Fulton, *Trayvon: Ten Years Later*.

Chapter 7

1. Scott MacFarlane and Cassidy McDonald, "Jan. 6 Timeline: Key Moments from the Attack on the Capitol," January 6, 2023, CBS News, https://www.cbsnews.com/live-updates/jan-6-capitol -riot-timeline-key-moments/.
2. Quotes from Shaye Moss and Ruby Freeman throughout this chapter were found at "Special Series: House Jan. 6 Committee Hearings," NPR, accessed July 28, 2023, https://www.npr.org /series/1098490189/jan-6-subcommittee-hearings.
3. "Changing Names," Facing History & Ourselves, May 12, 2020, https://www.facinghistory.org/resource-library/changing-names.
4. Marie Benedict and Victoria Christopher Murray, *The Personal Librarian* (New York: Penguin Publishing, 2021).
5. "Sojourner Truth," African American Odyssey, accessed July 28, 2023, https://www.loc.gov/exhibits/odyssey/educate/truth .html.

Chapter 8

1. Leymah Gbowee, *Mighty Be Our Powers: How Sisterhood, Prayer, and Sex Changed a Nation at War* (New York: Beast Books, 2011), Location #122, Kindle edition.
2. Gbowee, Location #129, Kindle edition.

3. Gbowee, Location #143, Kindle edition.
4. Gbowee, Location #164, Kindle edition.

Chapter 9

1. Craig S. Keener, *The IVP Bible Background Commentary: New Testament* (Downers Grove, IL: InterVarsity Press, 2014), 370.
2. Keener, *IVP Bible Background Commentary: New Testament*, 369.
3. ACLU of Northern CA, "From Enslaved to Entrepreneur: The Biddy Mason Story," YouTube, November 10, 2019, https://www.youtube.com/watch?v=kmt6hK4Y4sU.
4. "From Enslaved to Entrepreneur," ACLU of Northern California, accessed July 28, 2023, https://www.aclunc.org/sites/goldchains/explore/biddy-mason.html.
5. Kristen Jordan Shamus, "How a Freed Slave Made It into the Michigan Women's Hall of Fame," *Detroit Free Press*, July 23, 2017, https://www.freep.com/story/life/family/kristen-jordan-shamus/2017/07/24/elizabeth-denison-forth-michigan-womens-hall-fame-slavery/485819001/.
6. Jacqueline L. Tobin, *From Midnight to Dawn: The Last Tracks of the Underground Railroad* (New York: Doubleday, 2007), x.
7. Brett Kast, "'Lisette' Denison Forth Went from Slavery in Metro Detroit to Owning Land, Building a Church," WXYZ Detroit, February 24, 2022, https://www.wxyz.com/news/black-history-month/lisette-denison-forth-went-from-slavery-in-metro-detroit-to-owning-land-building-a-church.
8. Last Will and Testament of Lisette Denison Forth, 1866.

Chapter 10

1. Birger A. Pearson, "From Saint to Sinner," *Bible Review*, Spring 2005.
2. James Carroll, "Who Was Mary Magdalene?," *Smithsonian*, June 2006, https://www.smithsonianmag.com/history/who-was-mary-magdalene-119565482/.
3. Jane Schaberg, *The Resurrection of Mary Magdalene: Legends, Apocrypha, and the Christian Testament* (New York: Continuum, 2002), 8.
4. *Hidden Figures*, directed by Theodore Melfi (Levantine Films and Chernin Entertainment, 2017).
5. Margot Lee Shetterly, *Hidden Figures: The American Dream and the Untold Story of the Black Women Mathematicians Who Helped Win the Space Race* (New York: William Morrow, 2016), 223.

6. Shetterly, *Hidden Figures*, 222.
7. Henry Louis Gates Jr., *Life upon These Shores: Looking at African American History* (New York: Knopf, 2011), 236.
8. Ida E. Jones, "Mary McLeod Bethune, True Democracy, and the Fight for Universal Suffrage," *Women's Suffrage Centennial Commission* (blog), National Park Service, December 14, 2020, https://www.nps.gov/articles/000/mary-mcleod-bethune-true -democracy-and-the-fight-for-universal-suffrage.htm.
9. "Dr. Mary McLeod Bethune," Volusia County Florida, accessed July 28, 2023, https://www.volusia.org/residents/history /volusia-stories/dr-mary-mcleod-bethune.stml.
10. Martha S. Jones, "Mary McLeod Bethune Was at the Vanguard of More Than 50 Years of Black Progress," *Smithsonian*, July 2020, https://www.smithsonianmag.com/history/mary-mcleod -bethune-vanguard-more-than-50-years-black-progress -180975202/.
11. Mary Bethune, "Dr. Bethune's Last Will & Testament," Bethune-Cookman University, accessed July 31, 2023, https://www .cookman.edu/history/last-will-testament.html.
12. Amelia Mason, "Harriet Powers' Quilts Leave a Complicated Legacy for Her Descendent," WBUR, January 24, 2022, https://www.wbur.org/news/2022/01/24/harriet-powers-quilts -descendent.
13. "Black History and Quilting, a Story," African American Registry, March 18, 2023, https://aaregistry.org/story/black-history -and-quilting-a-brief-story/.
14. Mason, "Harriet Powers' quilts leave a complicated legacy."
15. Stevie Chick, "'She Told Martin Luther King: Tell 'Em about the Dream!' The Eternal Life of Gospel Singer Mahalia Jackson," *Guardian*, May 19, 2022, https://www.theguardian.com/music /2022/may/19/mahalia-jackson-martin-luther-king-al-sharpton.
16. Mark Burford, *Mahalia Jackson and the Black Gospel Field* (New York: Oxford University Press, 2019), 13.
17. Burford, *Mahalia Jackson and the Black Gospel Field*, 13.
18. Burford, *Mahalia Jackson and the Black Gospel Field*, 14.
19. The official website of the Mahalia Jackson residual family corporation, http://www.mahaliajackson.us/biography/.
20. Crystal Shaw-King, "How Cathy Hughes Took a Dream, Faith and Her Blessings to Build Success," *Ebony*, February 23, 2017, https://www.ebony.com/cathy-hughes-tvone-media/.
21. Dennis Herrick, *Media Management in the Age of Giants: Business Dynamics of Journalism* (Albuquerque: University of New Mexico Press, 2012), 43.
22. Cathy Hughes, "That's the Reason I Believe in the Power of

Prayer," AZQuotes, accessed July 31, 2023, https://www
.azquotes.com/quote/1363955.

23. Gabrielle Douglas and Michelle Burford, *Grace, Gold, and
Glory: My Leap of Faith* (Grand Rapids, MI: Zonderkidz, 2012),
Location #10, Kindle edition.

24. Douglas and Burford, *Grace, Gold, and Glory*, Location #23,
Kindle edition.

25. Douglas and Burford, *Grace, Gold, and Glory*, Locations
#187–88, Kindle edition.

26. Latasha Morrison, *Be the Bridge: Pursuing God's Heart for
Racial Reconciliation* (New York: Waterbrook, 2019), Location
#5, Kindle edition.

27. Morrison, *Be the Bridge*, Location #7, Kindle edition.

28. Morrison, *Be the Bridge*, Location #6, Kindle edition.

29. Morrison, *Be the Bridge*, Location #9, Kindle edition

30. Morrison, *Be the Bridge*, Location #8, Kindle edition.

Epilogue

1. *Beloved*, directed by Jonathan Demme (Touchstone Pictures and
Harpo Films, 1998). Based on the book *Beloved* by Toni Morrison.

See Us.

Hear Us.

Experience VOICES.

VOICES amplifies the strengths, struggles, and courageous faith of Black image bearers of God.

Podcasts, blogs, books, films, and more . . .

Find out more at **experiencevoices.org**